# Representative Bureaucracy

## SAMUEL KRISLOV
*University of Minnesota*

PRENTICE-HALL, INC., ENGLEWOOD CLIFFS, N.J.

Library of Congress Cataloging in Publication Data

Krislov, Samuel.
    Representative bureaucracy.

    Bibliography: p.
    1. Bureaucracy. 2. Representative government and
representation. 3. Representative government and
representation—United States. I. Title.
JF1411.K74        320.4        73-21814
ISBN   0-13-773747-5

REPRESENTATIVE BUREAUCRACY
was originally planned as part of the
Foundations of Public Administration Series,
the editor of which was the late Wallace S. Sayre.

© 1974 by
Prentice-Hall, Inc., Englewood Cliffs, N.J. 07632

10 9 8 7 6 5 4 3 2 1

*Prentice-Hall International, Inc., London
Prentice-Hall of Australia, Pty. Ltd., Sydney
Prentice-Hall of Canada, Ltd., Toronto
Prentice-Hall of India Private Limited, New Delhi
Prentice-Hall of Japan, Inc., Tokyo*

# Acknowledgments

This book germinated from the inspired graduate teaching of William Ebenstein at Princeton, who prodded us to explore byways we thought were dull—administration, economics, and other stuff like that. It took shape in discussions with Einar Hardin and Herbert Garfinkel at Michigan State University's Center for Labor and Industrial Relations. Its first fruits were due to the help of Herbert Hill and the late Arthur Ross.

The encouragement of the publisher of *The Negro in Federal Employment*, the University of Minnesota Press, and that of my friends, Harold Chase, David Fellman, and the late Wallace Sayre (a truly gentle man), helped me to continue developing these ideas and concepts through several years of close association.

The Ford Foundation, through a Ford Faculty Fellowship for 1972–73, made the writing of this volume and related publications possible.

All readers are hereby warned that I expect to continue working along these lines, even without further urging. For that and any other failings I am responsible and assume all blame.

iii

To my colleagues at the University of Minnesota,
Department of Political Science—

"Wherever you are it is your own friends
who make your world."

**William James**

# Contents

## 3 Why Bureaucracies Can Never Be Fully Representative    42

## 4 How Bureaucracies Can (and Should) Be Representative    63

# Introduction

When this book began to take form, its topic—representative bureaucracy—was, at least in terms of general concern, of remote though hardly inconsequential importance. In recent months it has emerged among those who consider public policy as one of the bitterest and most discussed issues. The questions of quotas, of the merit of "compensatory justice," or (as I shall argue) of "remedial steps" have evoked much heated debate.

In many ways the light thrown on the subject has been dispropor-tionately small. The reasons are not hard to find. Both sides feel there is an advantage in exaggeration and strongly stated positions, but these political techniques do tend to blur the fine points of the issues. This is borne out by a refreshingly candid comment by Christopher Jencks:

> For analytic purposes, it is therefore useful to distinguish between "equal opportunity" (i.e., treating everyone alike) and "compensatory opportunity" (i.e., helping the neediest). Unfortunately, conceptual clarity is precisely what the advocates of compensatory opportunity (including ourselves) feel they cannot

afford. "Compensatory opportunity" is a slogan devoid of political appeal, while "equal opportunity" is still capable of rallying widespread support. Advocates of compensatory opportunity have therefore felt obliged to pretend that "equal opportunity" really implies compensatory opportunity. We see no reason for abandoning this sleight of hand, but it is also useful to recognize that treating everyone alike is not the same as helping the neediest.[1]

Similarly, those who are critical of what they see as a drive toward quotas as the system of selection throughout society tend to argue in terms of extreme examples as though these were the everyday standard. To the argument that these are untypical, such critics answer in terms of Alfred North Whitehead's "emergents"—the untypical is what is in process of becoming the general.

The issues of equality, merit, and reward are at the heart of current ideological conflict. One is as amused as amazed to read John Kenneth Galbraith's 1958 observation that "while it continues to have a large ritualistic role in the conventional wisdom of conservatives and liberals, inequality has ceased to preoccupy men's minds." [2] It is precisely as a preoccupation that it has survived. Irving Kristol has suggested that the shibboleths of inequality are used by elite "intellectuals" to attack bourgeois society; the real intention is not to elevate the poor so much as to demean the businessman and thus confirm the position of the snobbish counterculture. So, he argues, the criticism will perversely increase even as actual inequality wanes. Whether or not Kristol has accurately depicted the motives, it is clear that at the core of the ideological unity currently distinguishing the left in western society is the issue of inequality. It is, to employ an overused analogy, something of a secular religion, evoking devotion, sacrifice, and intensity.

The present study deals with these problems in terms of one set of social institutions—the public bureaucracy—and in terms of a single claim—to societal representativeness—offsetting those of "presumed merit" and "job-skill-related" criteria.

Part of the process of obfuscation has been the insistence of partisans that the issues can be clearly drawn on matters such as the above. This volume will acknowledge throughout the complexity involved in just such concepts—a complexity outlined in *The Negro in Federal Employment*.[3] It is perhaps wise to recapitulate and expand that argument here.

The fundamental fallacy encouraged by the practitioners of public and other "scientific" administration is that job analysis is possible for most if not all of the positions in our society. The implicit models are elemental jobs, e.g.,

---

[1] Christopher Jencks, *Inequality* (New York: Basic Books, 1972), p. 75.

[2] John K. Galbraith, *The Affluent Society* (Cambridge, Mass.: Houghton Mifflin, 1958), p. 82.

[3] Samuel Krislov, *The Negro in Federal Employment* (Minneapolis, Minn.: University of Minnesota Press, 1967).

working on an assembly line or such powerful and seductive examples as that of the surgeon who literally can or cannot "cut it."

Of course it is realized that any particular sample of ability—one day's effort, for example—is subject to error. The reliability of this kind of sample is in addition generally aggravated by the need to pick some surrogate for the requisite ability such as a paper and pencil test. In all of this it is assumed that there is a generally agreed-upon definition of what ideally should be measured.

In fact, the complexity far exceeds these obvious points. Expanding Blau—who in turn builds on Talcott Parsons and Robert F. Bales—I have suggested that merit and the criteria for selection and promotion can be approached as a series of "nesting" concepts with their appropriateness a matter of perspectives. In this sense, there are "multiple realities" in which criteria not only become less precise but encompass wider and wider viewpoints of what is an appropriate consideration.

Thus a surgeon's ability to diagnose is at least a second dimension of competence. His or her skill at organizing an office and the operating room team is even less esteemed, and yet it may be very consequential. The human relations involved in dealings with nurses may affect both the operation conditions and the aftercare, which is a significant aspect of the entire medical treatment—especially in cases such as the treatment of ulcers where poor attitudes transmitted to the patient can be immediately related to the recurrence of problems. The perennial TV plot involving the extraoperating room activity of the doctor who offends the clinic patron—usually by political or romantic activity—illustrates another set of problems complicating the supposedly simple job analysis. In fact, personal activities well beyond the simple task performance do impinge on successful operations of an institution. I am aware of an instance where a full-time administrator had to be hired to cope with the many-faceted activities of an inspiring and inspired idea man who didn't always observe the niceties of university rules before making what sometimes proved to be embarrassing commitments. There are extra costs that may result when one or more other physicians have to give up time that would otherwise be devoted to patients in order to rule on ethical questions, mediate, soothe ruffled feelings, or raise funds to substitute for sums lost through another's rudeness.

From the patient's viewpoint, only one set of considerations seems relevant—those that improve his care. From the standpoint of the physician's colleagues, fair use of nurses' time and such contributions as improvement of others' skill through keen analysis and awareness of new literature loom as worthy of consideration. The hospital administrator may value the individual who works well with others; the immediate community may esteem the TV celebrity; and society at large may value most the surgeon whose discoveries lead to further progress. All these perspectives are legitimate within their given context.

The point can be generalized. It is not simply that the physician's position, nominally the quintessence of a specific skill-oriented job, has complex ramifications. Rather, parallel observations can be made of the typical undergraduate's view of the professor as classroom teacher, the graduate student's emphasis on his creative helpfulness, the college's emphasis on his scholarship and the enhancement of departmental reputation, and his chairman's concern for his administrative contribution.

It is this multiple perspective that justifies "bumping," the practice of allowing unneeded employees in one office to displace employees with less seniority in another office. From the standpoint of the larger bureaucratic structure it is seen as a generalized procedure that helps induce everyone, including other members of the unit, adversely affected by the "bumping" to join and stay with the service, and to have some confidence in career lines. Similarly—and in a sense more grandiosely—veteran's preference is justified on the grounds that the soldier's defense of the social system is a prerequisite to the bureaucratic structure, and therefore a logical necessity for maintaining the operation as a whole.

The unfolding of such concepts is rather like an onion or artichoke in its nature. Essentially, taking a broader view is the assimilation of apparently extrinsic standards, which from the new perspective is quite reasonable and very much in order.

In short there is no natural dividing line between intrinsic and extrinsic criteria. And oddly enough, this makes it imperative that a line be drawn. If an institution is to perform its task, it must as a rule exclude external considerations that impinge on its own integrity. Such considerations as "private lives" or "non-job-connected background characteristics" are in modern and most premodern structures rigorously excluded from evaluation on the somewhat specious grounds that they do not affect performance—though they often do—or that they can be regulated through monitoring of performance—though performance is only crudely monitored in fact, and these criteria are realistically most relevant at point of hiring.

The tension between sets of criteria is greatest in connection with public service. On the one hand, the multiple perspectives, the variety of groupings that must be satisfied, is at maximum with respect to societally determined positions. A public office makes for public fuss. The process of preferring one or another set of criteria is one of policy making, of agenda setting, of preference ordering, of cue giving for the other sectors as well. Furthermore, the public sector has explicit need for extrinsic validation. A major task of governance is to gain support for policies. No matter how brilliantly conceived, no matter how artfully contrived, government action usually also requires societal support. And one of the oldest methods of securing such support is to draw a wide segment of society into the government to convey and to merchandise a policy.

Scholars in developmental administration have had to expand their concepts of administrative effectiveness to talk about "penetration," that is, the degree to which a government is able to move its policies into action outside the government halls. They were led to the concept by examination of former colonial civil services that continued to maintain their technical internal efficiency, but, having lost external military leverage, were increasingly ignored, isolated, and ineffectual. In most instances this was in part a product of the narrow base from which the colonial powers generally drew their native pen bearers. (The British often deliberately played off segments of society and entrusted bureaucratic power to groups heavily dependent on their foreign masters, for example, the Copts in Egypt. Such minorities were unlikely to seek or achieve independent power.)

All in all then, the pressure on government service to accommodate a wide variety of nontask considerations is great. But the threat of succumbing to the pressures, of sacrificing capacity to act, is also evident. While governments, like all institutions, succumb to pressures and trade off various boons for social peace, they are more vulnerable than many other institutions in that they act more publicly. This is especially true of Western democracies but is in essence true of all governments. The process of political selection is, other factors being equal, more open and deemed more a matter of general concern than, say, industrial recruitment. Special treatment for one group generates demands from other groups. (This is a group analogy with Ambrose Bierce's definition of patronage as the process of creating nine enemies and one ingrate.) Multiple effects from officially stated public policy can be salutary, or at least can be, as some have argued, the geometric diffusion of mediocrity.

This volume seeks to evaluate and mediate such claims regarding the public service, not in the popular terms of discourse, but in the light of the application of a quite different principle, that of "representative bureaucracy." That term suggests that administrative structures might be characterized by the presence or absence of such representativeness, and the degree to which the structures have in fact been representative agencies.

In exploring these issues we approach the whole problem of legitimacy and authority in government. In avoiding current cant we can, perhaps, at least avoid falling into popular ruts and old clichés. It is perhaps too much to hope to avoid all the new ones.

It has generally been assumed that the American political system first developed the prototype of a mass bourgeois party. This in turn was widely diffused and also engendered the mass proletarian party (see, e.g., Maurice

Duverger).[4] It has also been suggested that the American bureaucracy was distinctive in its avoidance of class bias, and that this provides a unique opportunity for the radiating principle of representativeness to prevail.

The current argument has been less over this idealistic end than over means. To supporters of "guidelines" much of the argument is hypocritical or disguised racism; to critics the current effort is "reverse discrimination." By a more objective examination of the problem, I hope to clarify the issue and perhaps even to reconcile some of the differences among those of good will and fond hope. The sharing of world experience and historical perspective also seems to promise less heat and more light.

[4] Maurice Duverger, *Political Parties* (New York: John Wiley, 1954).

# 1

# Bureaucracy and Representation: Paradox Lost and Paradox Regained

## I. INTRODUCTION

The identification of bureaucracies with red tape and antagonism to the public is so ingrained that it is hard to think of their positive functions. To go further and consider such agencies as not merely executing clerical duties but as a contributing and positive component of the policy structure seems strange. As we shall argue in this chapter and throughout this volume, however, reflection points rather clearly in that direction. Bureaucracies make policy every day, sometimes in small ways, but quite as often in large ones. The effect of an administrative directive can be as far-reaching as a statute.

Who writes the directive—his or her style, values, concept of role—is as significant as who gets to be president, congressman, senator, member of parliament, or cabinet minister. The notion of representative bureaucracy is that broad social groups should have spokesmen and officeholders in administrative as well as political positions. The issue of the composition of a country's civil service is a basic one for political analysts and students as well as for citizens anxious to understand and activists interested in reform.

This chapter deals with a history of concern about bureaucracies—why it is that representativeness of bureaucracies has not been a social and analytic problem in the past, and why it seems relevant today. Indeed, this chapter suggests that bureaucratic representativeness lies very near the core of today's social and status problems.

## II.  BUREAUCRACIES:   MONSTERS OR SERVANTS?

Bureaucracies are things we may dislike but nevertheless always seem to have with us. On all sides—even in our political rhetoric—we constantly adopt the refrain: "Resolved: that government structures loom large, are growing, and should be curtailed." Yet the nature of our political demands, engendered by physical necessity, the proliferation of technology, and the pressures of population growth, contributes to the sustained growth, year after year, decade after decade, of the civil service.

In the American experience the bureaucracy has only reluctantly been allowed to grow. Edicts by the Executive and Congress to cut the civil service have been successful—if at all—only in slowing the rate of growth. For example, in September, 1950, Congress provided that all increases in personnel be temporary. When this proved ineffectual, the Jensen-Ferguson Amendment of 1951 introduced an arbitrary formula to limit the size of each agency. But in the face of the Amendment the civil service increased by 117,000 in a single year.[1] Another recent attempt, in conjunction with the 1968 Tax Surcharge Bill, saw the Bureau of the Budget limit new appointments to 70 to 75 percent of separations. Almost immediately Congress began exempting agencies from the rule. Before the year was out, one-third of all full-time employees were exempt and the guidelines were virtually nullified.[2]

This lack of approval and legitimacy for bureaucratic expansion has its functional uses, for otherwise public bureaucracies might expand almost without limit, since they do not have the need for economic justification that presumably limits the growth of private bureaucracies. A disapproving public which mistrusts good as well as bad administration seems to be the major—perhaps the only substantial—obstacle to indefinite expansion.

But this public disapproval of bureaucratic growth has its costs as well, for growth comes à la Topsy, without much planning or shaping. It is largely

[1] Paul Van Riper, *History of the United States Civil Service* (Evanston, Ill.: Row Peterson & Co., 1958), pp. 464–69.
[2] *Congressional Quarterly Almanac*, Vol. XXIV, 1968, p. 789.

unwanted and is popularly regarded as an inevitable evil beyond control or as something that may somehow get worse with attention.

The nature and composition of the bureaucracy comes into question mainly at times of crisis, and then usually as a response to some specific issue. A shortage of some skill, a crisis in confidence over the social class composition of a bureaucracy, or a public scandal may pinpoint an aspect of the question dealt with in this study to the detriment of the broader question of the composition of the bureaucracy as a whole.

That problem, which we shall discuss under the rubric of representative democracy, is the proper relationship of a bureaucracy to the broader social system. Is there any ideal relationship between the social composition of a society and that of its administrative units? Should a bureaucracy be in some sense representative of sectors of the system, as—in perhaps some more express way—we expect legislatures to be? To what extent, if any, is such a notion compatible with the more standard and professional values of efficiency and neutrality in political policy making? What values besides modish concern for ethnic proportionality would be served by such a policy? What functional needs constitute the possible boundaries of such a policy?

Similar questions are regularly asked about the so-called political organs of government. The information on the composition of legislatures is easily available, and the volitional, shaping role of the voter in their selection is obvious and even a praiseworthy aspect of good citizenship. But not only is it difficult to amass and digest information about the most active branch of American government—and in actual numbers virtually the totality—it is also assumed that when dealing with the administration in very real terms the job seeks the man, and that it is futile or worse to prescribe much about civil servants beyond a very vague minimum competence. These assumptions are usually examined only during a crisis of confidence.

This is notoriously such a time. The old ideological superstructures—the idealism and millenarianism of radical Marxism on the one hand and Pax Americana on the other—have lost most of their appeal, foundering on the use of force in Hungary, Czechoslovakia, and Vietnam. The diminishing of technocratic arguments even as they prevail is reflected in the retrenchment of doctrines of planning in the face of "Liebermanism" in the Soviet Union—that is to say return to more flexible market, capitalistlike arrangements—and in the shunning and denunciation of American expertise in the fields of housing and urban planning, welfare and social work, and foreign policy. (The classical denunciation is Noam Chomsky's *American Social Power and the New Mandarins*.)[3]

To a large extent these denunciations are the last flights of romanticism, or tiny correctives or epicycles to large-scale secular swings toward more

---

[3] Noam Chomsky, *American Social Power and the New Mandarins* (New York: Pantheon, 1969).

rather than less rationalization of society. The student revolt throughout the world—in Turkey, Japan, and Canada rather more fiercely than in the United States—emerges in large part as a Luddite effort to assert the force of sheer will, to replace, as one student leader put it, the "politics of the possible" with the "politics of the impossible." Even as each society has its Maoist fling, its assertion of the existentialist myth that man has no real limitations and that realities can be wished away, more hard-headed realists extend further their day-to-day control, whether they be Red Army men in China or computer-game-theorist-entrepreneurs and their government regulators in the United States. But at least their efforts are challenged and the assumptions of control examined as a result of these revolts.

## III.  KINGSLEY COINS (AND DISTORTS) A TERM

The term "representative bureaucracy" is generally attributed to J. Donald Kingsley. His book with that title appeared in 1944. Essentially, it argued for a liberalization of social class selection for the English bureaucracy. Beyond the novelty of an American writer finding some aspect of our system superior to that of the British civil service, Kingsley's book suggests—a bit weakly—that only a representative bureaucracy is likely to respond to changes in political currents. A nonrepresentative structure will sabotage the demands of a party whose program is at odds with the class from which the bureaucracy is drawn. But more concretely, Kingsley predicted the Labour party, if it came to power, would find the vaunted neutrality of British civil service a myth. However, his theoretical argument, expressed more in stray sentences than in a solidly developed thesis, suggests some more general issue was involved.

Kingsley had studied at the London School of Economics with William Robson and, more importantly, with Harold Laski. His view of English civil service follows their neo-Marxist lines. (Robson was a moderate Labourite, while Laski was an anti-Stalinist Marxist who in his later years believed more and more in the inevitability of revolution. Their analysis of the British civil service was, however, quite similar.) All three analysts interpreted bureaucratic structure along class lines. The old regime, Kingsley suggested, created an aristocratic feudal system based upon the eleemosynary concept of the civil service: the notion that key aristocratic families had the right to expect succor from adversity in the form of appointment to the public rolls.

> . . . it was this which led the crusading but anonymous author of the *Extraordinary Black Book* to complain that no one could obtain a position under Government who either lacked family influence or had been born in lawful wedlock. For those members of the aristocracy who "might otherwise fall into a

state that would inevitably bring disgrace upon rank" were frequently the feeble, the incompetent, or the illegitimate.[4]

It was against this feudalistic holdover that the Northcote-Trevelyan Report of 1853 moved with all the moralistic force of bourgeois protest against privilege. And in the view of our analysts these efforts of two decades culminating in the Order in Council of 1870 created a new middle-class bureaucracy: "The modern official is indeed one of the outstanding creations of Victorian capitalist democracy; and without the civil and municipal services political democracy as we know it would be impossible." [5]

Not only did this act of creativity, as Kingsley shrewdly observed, help solve the constant middle-class problem of finding a respectable, gentlemanly occupation for the younger sons of the family; the establishment of a competitive public service also reflected new class interests as firmly as had the older system:

> Doubtless something more than a belief in the superiority of general over specialized training also contributed to the widespread acceptance of this doctrine when applied to the Civil Service. The "upper and middling" classes, through the public schools and the Universities, possessed a monopoly of such broad learning. . . . the effect of the Northcote-Trevelyan proposal for a division of labor in the Service between intellectual and routine work and for separate systems of recruitment based upon that division, was a further guarantee of the social purity of the upper ranks of the Service. As Gladstone was quick to point out, this would give the gentlemanly class "command over all the higher posts," for the lower ranks would be a caste apart with different duties, different training, different prospects.[6]

Over the years two breaches in a strict caste system occurred. Promotions to the administrative class, though rare, were authorized and began to occur. Kingsley estimated these at about two a year out of 17,000 possible promotions.[7] Second, the rudiments of democratization of higher education meant that those with lower-class origins might well acquire the intellectual equipment necessary to pass the rigorous examinations. Like the first, the second breach was encouraged by official action, especially in reorganizations of the educational system. But to Kingsley these exceptions do not belie the broad truth as he sees it:

> Because equality of educational opportunity does not exist in England, the fact that the Service classes are linked to various rungs of the educational ladder

[4] J. Donald Kingsley, *Representative Bureaucracy* (Yellow Springs, Ohio: The Antioch Press, 1944), p. 27.
[5] William A. Robson, *The British Civil Servant* (London: G. Allen & Unwin, 1937), p. 12.
[6] Kingsley, *Representative Bureaucracy*, pp. 69–70.
[7] Kingsley, *Representative Bureaucracy*, pp. 248–49.

means that each is drawn pretty largely from a distinct stratum of society. It is as unusual for the son of a working class parent to find his way into the Administrative Class as it is for the son of the well-to-do to become a clerk at the bottom. Both cases may, in fact, occur, but such exceptions do not imperil the generalization. To a remarkable degree each Service class is also a social class—a caste—and the service hierarchy pretty accurately mirrors the economic and social hierarchies outside.[8]

This creates a severe and critical challenge, as Kingsley sees it, for the bureaucracy threatens any proletarian-based program, and therefore constitutes a threat to true democratic options:

> There are obviously points beyond which a man cannot go in carrying out the will of another; and the fact that those limits have seldom been approached in the conduct of the Civil Service since 1870 bears witness to the unity of the middle class State. The convention of impartiality can be maintained only when the members of the directing grades of the Service are thoroughly committed to the larger purposes the State is attempting to serve; when, in other words, their views are identical with those of the dominant class as a whole. I have been at some pains to show that the achievement of such a basic unity was a principal object of middle class reform of the Civil Service and that the reforms of 1855 and 1870 were eminently successful in this respect. For the past seventy-five years, with very few exceptions, the leaders of all political parties and of the Civil Service have been united in regard to fundamentals. Their outlooks and points of view have been uniformly middle class and the identity of their fields of visions made a permanent Service a possible adventure.[9]

Kingsley's argument rests almost entirely on these thoughts, repeated again and again, all too often in identical words. Representative bureaucracy is necessary because there must be at least some administrators sympathetic to the programmatic concerns of the dominant political party. He seems oblivious to virtually any other ramifications of the argument for representativeness and indeed his argument would seem better suited to a straightforward defense of the class basis of government. Given his view of human nature and the impossibility of political neutrality, a proletarian political majority would seem to require not proportionate representation of proletarians but an even more extensive control. The dawning era of Labour power would require a class instrumentality, just as in the past. In that view, Labour would presumably create its own instrumentality with new means of control as well as a drastic revision in recruitment patterns. But Kingsley, coauthor of a standard book on personnel selection, merely urges reform of caste selection processes. His efforts to weld a crude Marxist historical view to an American

[8] Kingsley, *Representative Bureaucracy*, p. 148.
[9] Kingsley, *Representative Bureaucracy*, p. 278.

public-administration emphasis on individual merit is not only unsuccessful and unconvincing—it seems to have been a product of little thought, a reflex action to the situation of the times.

Kingsley's almost somnambulistic—and, as I shall argue, obfuscating—posing of a truly seminal question is partly redeemed by his few pages on the question of women's rights. Where traditional Marxist formula explanations are not at hand, Kingsley is free to offer other explanations. And his indictment of sex discrimination is really at variance with the single-mindedness of the rest of his treatment, because it recognizes factors other than class:

> . . . it is precisely because the female administrator is so exceptional and because women do not enjoy with men equality of opportunity inside, or outside, the service that the continuance of such a condition is, it seems to me, antipathetic to any political democracy. The democratic State cannot afford to exclude any considerable body of its citizens from full participation in its affairs. It requires at every point that superior insight and wisdom which is the peculiar product of the pooling of diverse streams of experience. In this lies the strength of representative government. Upon it depends the superiority of the democratic Civil Service over its totalitarian rivals. In a democracy competence alone is not enough. The public service must also be representative if the State is to liberate rather than to enslave.[10]

So Kingsley notes the linkage between modes of participation allowed a group and its attitudes toward power and social policy, a linkage we shall stress later. The handful of pages on sex discrimination in *Representative Bureaucracy* constitute a redeeming aspect in that they venture beyond the monotonous emphasis of the rest of the volume. They give Kingsley the right not only to claim coining a term, but also suggest the road to a fuller analysis of the problem involved.

## IV.  THE PROBLEM LOOMS MUCH LARGER THAN CLASS ORIGIN

It is most doubtful that posing the analysis of representative bureaucracy in terms of social class was to hit at even the most significant aspect of the problem. What is clear is that such a concentration of focus trivialized a question which to this time has not been adequately treated.

On the simplest level of political prophecy, the Kingsley-Laski predictions seem today remotely archaic and even a bit fatuous. The postwar Attlee Labour government simply did not experience the bureaucratic resistance they anticipated. The testimony of Sidney Webb and George

---

[10] Kingsley, *Representative Bureaucracy*, p. 185.

Lansbury,[11] among others, about the interwar Labourite regimes indicates a similar experience. But Kingsley dismissed that evidence inasmuch as no truly socialist measures had been pressed by the MacDonald cabinet. Robson had suggested that the cooperation in the MacDonald era left something lacking; but his statements are not overwhelmingly persuasive:

> There were numerous instances where members of the Labour governments of 1924 and 1929 felt intimidated and overshadowed by the superior training and manners of their chief officials. It is a short step from intimidation to resentment.[12]

Herbert Morrison is unequivocal on this matter, however, and his is the last word. Speaking as one who served in both MacDonald's and Attlee's cabinets, Morrison noted:

> The belief among some of the public and even some Members of Parliament that civil servants do not work in harmony with Ministers I have hardly ever found to be justified. . . . What the reader can be sure of is that the British Civil Service is loyal to the Government of the day. The worst that can be said of them is that sometimes they are not quick enough in accustoming themselves to new ideas, but then it is up to the Minister to educate them. The greatest danger in the running of a Government Department is a Minister who does not know how to handle civil servants.[13]

Labourite experience of the devotion of the bureaucracy to the guidelines set by the cabinet was so favorable that the topic was not even broached when Harold Wilson's government took office in 1964.

In the intervening years, particularly as a consequence of reforms in the educational system, the bureaucracy has moved toward representativeness as urged by the Labourites. In this period the political leadership of the Labour Party has also begun to resemble the structure of other British elites—including that of the Conservative Party. The middle-class, and occasionally upper-class, leadership of Labour no longer is really anomalous, so that Labour politicians and Treasury representatives can sit down together with hardly a proletarian among them.[14]

All of this reflects the artificial nature of much of the discussion of social class origins of officeholders. By and large, once civil servants take office, they

---

[11] Seymour Martin Lipset, *Agrarian Socialism* (Berkeley: University of California Press, 1950), p. 259.

[12] Robson, *The British Civil Servant*, p. 18.

[13] Herbert Morrison, *Government and Parliament* (London: Oxford University Press, 1954), pp. 334–36.

[14] See, e.g., W. L. Guttsman, "Changes in British Labor Leadership," in *Political Decision Makers*, ed. Dwaine Marvick (Beverly Hills, Calif.: Glencoe Press, 1961), pp. 91–137.

do so with at least middle-class skills and assume, if they do not have it already, at least middle-class status. Those in the leadership strata of any social group are not average, at least in some sense. Even if a system were organized to deny administrators pecuniary benefits and material comforts, the status accorded them would almost certainly elevate them from the mass. Indeed, most socialist theorists accorded leadership tasks even higher honor, to compensate for withdrawal of fiscal advantage so that there might be increased emphasis on distinctive status in a less materialistic society.

What is discussed in terms of social class of officeholders is in fact not usually the social class of the incumbents but rather their social origins. There is no doubt some significance in the relationship between the two, but they are hardly the same. How one views the social class of one's father varies from person to person; there is not even the statistical predictability that attaches to current class affiliations—itself a notoriously tricky category. Reviewing the bureaucracy's representativeness as far as social origins is concerned tells us something about class mobility in the society. It tells us very little about what Kingsley suggests is his primary concern—the capacity of the administrative structure to respond to the political climate or its representativeness as to social attitudes. People who have recently risen in status have constituted one of the bulwarks of the worst kinds of reaction almost as often as such individuals have been the sources of forward thought.

Kingsley's error—and this criticism may be generalized to most users of social origin analysis—is in confusing two divergent notions of representativeness. I have previously treated these two notions in dealing with another institutional pattern:

> Evidence on the background characteristics . . . casts some light on the sharing of power and responsibility of various groupings in our society and raises some questions as to whether this is a proper, desirable, and effective distribution. This is the representational question. There is also the question of the relation between . . . background and . . . effectiveness. This can be dubbed the functional problem.[15]

In general, studies have emphasized ad nauseam the disproportionate participation in bureaucracy of sons and daughters of middle-class parents.[16] This study will dwell from time to time on this aspect of the problem, but it will also reflect a feeling that the focus is misplaced. The thesis on this point is that bureaucracies are by their nature middle-class in skills and needs. Fundamentally, these skills must be rewarded in special ways to generate

---

[15] Samuel Krislov, *The Supreme Court in the Political Process* (New York: Macmillan, 1965), p. 30.

[16] The most comprehensive and thoughtful of these is V. Subramaniam, "Representative Bureaucracy: A Reassessment," *American Political Science Review*, LXI, December (1967), 1010–19.

their availability. Since in every known modern society social position is in large part a function of family opportunity, bureaucracies will reflect this relationship. In no society can it be said that the social class of its present members is randomly associated with that of their parents. Therefore, we can expect to find a disproportionate number of occupants of any middle-class role to have parents who were also middle class. To draw conclusions about accessibility to a particular role we would generally require comparative data about other middle-class positions or longitudinal data about the particular slot. Failing that, evidence about parentage tells us more about the rate of upward social mobility in a society than it does about the operational characteristics of the society.

Presumably it is the latter issue that is at stake. We want to know about the actual behavior of individuals and aggregates. We can, by and large, tease out some fairly reliable generalizations about behavior if we know the regular, everyday behavioral characteristics of large numbers of people. We can then generalize with fair accuracy about some specific percentage of the larger group. Group affiliations in short can operate as indexes of political beliefs.

It is very doubtful that parental social origins operate this way. A man who rises to the top may in his beliefs be excessively diffident or cocksure, inclined to help the underdog, or feel everyone should emulate his achievement. By and large, it is the way he and others in society view his rise that is significant, and better indexes to these points of view are available than those of parental origin.

At best an examination of the social origins of bureaucrats can only provide indirect evidence for the question of the representative character of the bureaucracy. A man's origins, his birthmarks, have little to do with his adult abilities. They tell very little about how he will approach his task, and are inadequate even as evidence of how others will regard his actions as ones they would also take.

Both aspects of the issue contain genuine (as well as merely plausible) problems that demand further analysis. Social class is but one of the least of these. Kingsley, we noted, devoted some attention to sex discrimination, and there are occasional signs of concern about the necessary range of skills for the operation of the bureaucracy. Even more significant questions—race, language and ethnicity on the one hand, personality types on the other—were not so important in a study focused on relatively homogeneous Britain.

When Kingsley wrote, Laski had already for decades been raising the question with his Indian students of their participation in administration. Observers had indeed noted the preoccupation of colonials with bureaucratic office, and had characterized it as being even more central to their concern than party and political reform. Throughout the British Empire the natives were restlessly pursuing their claim to self-administration or at least to participation in the administration of their country.

The raising of the issue of native administration by colonial intellectuals was the complement to the early struggles over administrative participation. T. B. Macaulay for all his contempt of Eastern culture had drafted clause 87 of the East India Charter Act of 1833 and thus had helped put into the statute books the equal right of all races to serve in the colonial civil service. Macaulay took great pride in this policy, which was officially reiterated by Queen Victoria when in 1858 the Crown succeeded the East India Company as ruler of India. Bureaucratic representation by Indians was expressly urged as mitigation for the absence of popular institutions. But even under the Company this policy was nullified in practice on the scene as regulations from the home office (probably drafted by another great name in classic English liberalism, James Mill) were put aside. As Benjamin Jowett expressly and openly recognized in 1854, by limiting colonial participation in higher administration, England would be assuring her Oxford students desirable positions. Ironically, the desire for the same type of status by colonial intellectuals—often trained by Laski at the London School of Economics— was to be one of the major driving forces in the colonial drive for independence from Great Britain almost precisely a century later.[17] They were magnificently aware of the hypocrisy of the British profession of openness of the system while they engaged in such practices as continually lowering the maximum age for recruitment—to take advantage of the difficulties involved in colonials getting an English education. The maximum age for entering the service in India, for example, was originally twenty-three, then in 1861 lowered to twenty-one, and in 1876 to nineteen. The effect was that Indians would have had to go to England by age fifteen to get their college training.[18]

Control of bureaucracy by an outside power added another complication. It was often in the ruler's interest to set one social group against another. The British, it has been suggested by many, were past masters at this. In various societies they favored highly literate minorities with little social leverage who would be loyal creatures of the imperial power—precisely as predicted by Max Weber. Thus, Copts, Chinese, Parsees, and others were disproportionately drawn into their Majesties' Service in various parts of the Empire. But groups with social power, in turn, tried to modify these arrangements and secure definite commitments to protect their rights. Thus, community representation and quotas of a direct or veiled nature were commonplace arrangements.

[17] See Richard Symonds, *The British and Their Successors* (London: Faber and Faber, 1966), pp. 16, 18, 28–39, and 44.
[18] Hugh Tinker, "Structure of the British Imperial Heritage," in *Asian Bureaucratic Systems Emergent from the British Imperial Tradition*, ed. Ralph Braibanti (Durham, N.C.: Duke University Press, 1966), pp. 25, 26, 54, and 55.

So long as they were colonial possessions, these issues were merely part of the struggle for independence. Independence then called attention to the issues of broad bureaucratic participation in newly established countries and the adjudication of claims of differing internal groups to office. Their past sensitization to discrimination, the need for employment for the educated, and the heightened self-consciousness of the different communities induced by the practice of most imperial powers made representation a most salient issue. This in turn called attention to a wide range of parallel problems in better-established countries—problems which are in fact closely related and which are best treated under this common heading, the issue of bureaucratic representation.

## V.  THE EMERGENCE OF THE ISSUE IN AMERICAN SOCIETY

The issue of representative bureaucracy has, of course, been dramatized by the issue of Black rights in the United States; the Blacks were quickly joined in their demands by Puerto Ricans, Chicanos, and women. For Americans, as well as for foreign observers of the American scene, this has become a seminal challenge to the American dream.

How we solve the problem of Black participation in power and Black sharing of status and goods in American society will have a great effect on our self-image as well as on the image we project abroad. The American dream was built on several major themes, but its dominant one was its ability to cope effectively with diversity in society. The claim of a capacity to deal with intergroup conflicts that were in their native setting irrepressible lay at the heart of the romantic notion of America as the new-found and innocent land that could be a model for the world. Not shackled by the disabilities of the old feudal system, and freed from traditions of conflicts and feuds, American society was to be the paradigm for future societies of promise and worth—a United States of Europe, of Asia, of Africa, of the world itself.

This dream has taken sharply divergent forms without shattering that essential faith. The original notion was the "melting pot" concept made famous by Israel Zangwill.[19] The "tempest-tossed" and "homeless" were all tossed into the cauldron of American life and their dross thrown off, their character reformed. In this sociological equivalent of America's political motto of *E Pluribus Unum,* a common life-style and character were the expected result from this tempering process.

Horace Kallen's more complex program of "cultural pluralism" echoed William James's plea: "pluralism lets things really exist in the each-form or

---

[19] Israel Zangwill, *The Melting Pot* (New York: Macmillan, 1913).

distributively. Monism thinks that the all-form or collective unit is the only form that is rational." [20] Kallen suggested that a polyglot culture would in fact be stronger than any enforced conformity. Kallen's arguments became the standard claim for unity-in-diversity—tolerating, even celebrating, the distinctiveness of subgroups as contributing to a synthesizing realization of the whole person as an American.[21]

This later version—a product of post–World War I days—had even greater attraction than the earlier program. The melting pot requires not just the taking on of a new identity but rejection of the old. The "cultural pluralistic" notion is not a jealous god, and rather resembles oriental religions that allow continued obeisance to the old, while granting absolution for accepting the new. Throughout the world the claim for social pluralism, perhaps in a politically federal system, has emerged as a potential solution to ethnic, religious, or local animosities, short of "final solutions" of physical or cultural annihilation.

The failure of American society over two centuries to deal with its indigenous Indian and forcibly imported Black populations became salient. In the nineteenth century they were excludable as "the troublesome presence," as President Grant so gracefully put it.[22] They were the essence of the problem, the proof of the pudding, in the twentieth century.

Whether it was this externally obvious contradiction, or the inexorable influence of the "American dilemma," the patent affront to our conscience noted by Gunnar Myrdal, or the changing geographic, political, economic, and educational status of the Negro, this past quarter-century has been marked by an extensive governmental, private, and morally directed effort to end this profound anomaly in our democratic order.

In this effort, governmental service has been important as both a symbol and a cause. As a major vehicle of social change, the occupation of its positions by minority-group members has been significant in policy outcomes and in the subtle transactions that cumulatively constitute policy. Advances in this area have some of the character of showcase achievements, encouraging changes in career aspirations and patterns among the minority, and inspiring new efforts and goals for majority elites in the private sector.

This new look at the relationship of Blacks to public service has raised for a highly developed and presumably integrated society many of the same questions about government service raised in newly independent and/or less united systems. The questions then seem universal—perhaps, in reality, timeless.

[20] William James, *A Pluralistic Universe, Lecture 8* (New York: Longmans, Green and Co., 1909), p. 324.
[21] Horace Kallen, *Cultural Pluralism and the American Idea* (Philadelphia: University of Pennsylvania Press, 1956).
[22] See the book of that name by Eli Ginzberg and Alfred S. Eichner (New York: The Free Press, 1964).

The emergence of new states as a product of dissolution of older more comprehensive ones—from empire to nation, in Rupert Emerson's provocative epigraph—has hidden the need for creation of more comprehensive subunit communities. In this respect the newer states share to a remarkable degree the problems that the more established states have also ignored. The merging of dual societies or dual polities—often a subdominant one merged into partnership with a senior partner—is a continuous fact of modern society, and all too often a painful one. Northern Ireland, Belgium, Canada, and the United States have more in common with and more to learn from polyethnic, polyglot, or polydeist communities like Lebanon, India, and Malaysia than appears on the surface. And the bureaucracy with its manifold significance, its need for variety, and its large sample size is a better microcosm of the total society than more commonly studied areas such as legislatures and a better laboratory for studying broad political action.

## VI.  CONCLUSION AND SUMMARY

The concept of representative bureaucracy was originally developed to argue for a less elite, less class-biased civil service. As such it was hardly of great interest in the United States because this country's problem then was to develop a respected administrative structure that could attract elite groups. The bureaucracy has since gained in prestige and power. More significantly, our society now sees other lines of division—race, ethnicity, and sex—as becoming even more relevant than class. These new lines of division in turn have particular relevance to contemporary bureaucratic structures.

# 2

# Representativeness: The Emergence of the Concept and Its Dilemmas

## I. INTRODUCTION

The notion of representativeness has slowly permeated political thought. It is neither self-evident nor universal. Societies have functioned without it being considered a test of any institution; even when it has been accepted as applicable, differing, competing concepts of representativeness have been advocated.

In general, the appropriateness of representativeness has been most easily understood and accepted in conjunction with the exercise of policy judgment (as with legislatures or juries) and less with action and implementation (as with executives, judges, and administrators). Yet the notion is hardly remote to any bureaucracy, and the more rationalized and developed such structures have become, the more it seems appropriate. The greater the degree of discretion imputed to a bureaucracy, the more vigorous its functions, the stronger the need for the type of accountability and sense of responsibility implied by the call for representativeness. Indeed, the most important effects of representativeness may be the check exerted upon a bureaucracy when so constituted, and the trust made possible by the approximate identity of bureaucracy's interests with those of the general public.

## II. DEFINING OUR TERMS

To deal with the concept of representative bureaucracy requires some explication of terms. We shall for the moment at least be content with defining *bureaucracy* as the formal civil service of a political order. As Gaetano Mosca put it:

> The main characteristic of this type of social organization lies, we believe, in the fact that, wherever it exists, the central power conscripts a considerable portion of the social wealth by taxation and uses it first to maintain a military establishment and then to support a more or less extensive number of public services. The greater the number of officials who perform public duties and receive their salaries from the central government or from its local agencies, the more bureaucratic a society becomes.[1]

As is usually the case, the more familiar and seemingly easier-to-define term—*representation*—gives us more difficulty. (This might seem odd, but it follows because widely used terms usually acquire a range of connotations, so that more precise use requires delineation—in this case, *subtraction* of unnecessary meanings.) Representativeness means different things to different people and its employment with respect to the civil service presents an unfamiliar juxtaposition. In some ways the two notions clash, and constitute what the Greeks first called an *oxymoron*, the juncture of two contradictory notions to make a point, as in the phrases "deliberate speed" and "icy heat." The bureaucracy itself is anomalous in just this way, as suggested by the pregnant title of Eric Strauss's volume dealing with public administration, *The Ruling Servants*.[2] At times they are gray and timid, complaining of their inability to innovate or act. At other times, they seem both audacious and tenacious as in the French bureaucratic system which was essentially Napoleonic and has outlasted constitutional monarchs, several republics, a quisling regime, and a plebiscitary autocrat. Sometimes they combine these characteristics, as with the Weimar bureaucracy which hampered and humiliated the democratic government but collapsed before Nazi ruthlessness. But in any event it is clear they are no mere housekeepers. There is much of the Uriah Heep in the bureaucrat and he can assume authority, particularly in a vacuum.

[1] Gaetano Mosca, *The Ruling Class* (New York: McGraw-Hill, 1939), p. 83.
[2] See Eric Strauss, *The Ruling Servants* (New York: Praeger, 1961).

In the twentieth-century world it is clear that civil service has become more and more powerful, and, in close liaison with the operating executive, has been expansionist in its operations and its claims. Writing of the American situation Roger Davidson, for example, sees growing claims for the executive: "The conflict between Congress and the Executive can best be understood as a test of the representational capacities of these two institutions." [3] And his conclusion is clear: "In many respects, the civil service represents the American people more comprehensively than does Congress." [4]

That these claims seem strange reflects changes in the connotations of the word "representative" as it has been employed through the years. That evolution has been both historically inconsistent and gradual, so that pinpointing the time of changeover is impossible. It is an evolution over centuries, with a confused interrelationship of institutional and terminological change both of which have been largely independent, one from the other.

The simplest sense of representativeness is that of agency: a representative is one sent to make some specific representations. He has a job to do and is so authorized. The delegate notion is associated with political party control and majority rule. The most sophisticated concept is that of embodiment of will; the creature in miniature (or clearer, or quicker) form does precisely what the original body would have done. The difference is not merely that between a messenger sent for a specific purpose and an individual given general power of attorney. The advanced—almost metaphysical—notion of representation suggests additional legitimacy gained from some almost intuitive or random-sample isomorphism of the two bodies. The smaller represents—stands for—the larger because in some way it encapsulates—stands for—the larger. In between these notions are the more pragmatic assessments that officeholders are chosen originally because of a temporary or assumed identity of interests. The argument for periodic reelection, for example, rests upon the notion that divergence of views is more likely as time goes on. There are grave intellectual difficulties with each of these concepts. Perhaps this accounts for the cyclical, or even random, nature of the popularity of each.

The notion of identity of interests is both most ancient and highly contemporary. It partakes of primitive magic and mystical notions of incarnation, yet it is the basis of Rousseau's political philosophy and of fascistic ideology. Any concept of absolute identity of societal interests can be subjected to devastating criticism of the type in A. F. Bentley's *The Process of Government*.[5] The idea of isolated individuals pursuing discrete egoism simply cannot supply an adequate account of the creation of community.

[3] Roger H. Davidson, "Congress and the Executive: The Race for Representation," in *Congress: The First Branch of Government*, ed. A. DeGrazia (New York: Anchor, 1967), p. 365.

[4] Davidson, "Congress and the Executive: The Race for Representation," p. 383.

[5] Bentley, *The Process of Government* (Bloomington, Ind.: Principia Press, 1908, 1949).

The notion of group representation and delegation also contains fallacies as to the possibility of deducing group attitudes from leadership strata behavior, as Mancur Olson has cogently argued.[6] In a word, leaders often have separate interests. No pure theory of delegation can be justified on grounds of majority rule alone since anomalies in the system will always arise. The lifetime bureaucrat, the availability of other people's resources to leadership groups, and the differential access to information are more the rule than the exception.

Nor is this a totally unconscious policy. Most American legislators apparently hold to a pragmatic notion of their role, sometimes responding to opinion or to group pressures, sometimes following their own values. It is likely that gradations of attitudes within this consensus are more significant than the nominal agreement.[7]

## III.   WHAT DOES REPRESENTATION REQUIRE?

Closely allied to the relationship of the representative and the populace has been the question of caliber or type of individuals chosen for legislative positions. On the one hand, we may opt for the most capable of all—an option often, though not necessarily, linked to "virtual representation" or identity of interests notions. Conversely, we might logically seek microreproduction of the community, complete to representation of the feeble-minded and the underage. In practice, as C. K. Allen points out, real legislatures represent uneasy and changing accommodations between both types; representation is an amalgam of diversity with selection of above average but rarely exceptionally able individuals for this function of leadership.[8]

It is perhaps not surprising that practice shows no resolution of these matters; life has a way of blurring logical formulations. But there has also been little theoretical formulation; virtually all of it is little more than three centuries old. Carl Friedrich, in an authoritative discussion in the *Encyclopaedia Britannica*, suggests there was no need for earlier efforts since the simple structures of earlier governments required no rationalization.[9] This is hardly satisfying; many quite complex legislative and administrative structures—for example, in ancient China—existed long before modern times. The explanation would seem to lie rather in the lack of institutional conflict between such

[6] In Mancur Olson, *The Logic of Collective Action* (Cambridge, Mass.: Harvard University Press, 1965).

[7] See J. C. Wahlke and Heinz Eulau et al., *The Legislative System* (New York: Wiley, 1962). The overwhelming preference for one of their role choices suggests that refinement of breakdowns within it might be revealing.

[8] C. K. Allen, *Democracy and the Individual* (New York: Oxford University Press, 1943), pp. 21–22.

[9] "Bureaucracy," *Encyclopaedia Britannica* (1967), IV, 421–22.

representative institutions and the executive; conflicts were waged more in terms of replacement of specific individuals as monarchs or of replacement of specific subordinates than in terms of advocacy of regime or institutional change. Essentially all of the historically proliferating political structures seem to have been regarded as agencies of or subordinate to the ruler, while their occasional overt rebellions were principally justified in terms of some external higher moral principle, not in terms of the right of these officeholders to speak for others.

## IV. THE EMERGENCE OF THE MODERN REPRESENTATIVE AND BUREAUCRATIC STATE

Even when theoretical formulations for justifying political agencies did develop, no clean lines emerged. The political theory of representation, even legislative, is not impressive; that of administration is virtually nonexistent.

As is often the case, Max Weber's explanation of this history is rather more satisfying than more recent efforts. He suggests a typology similar to that developed above:

1. "Appropriated representation," an ancient form based principally on hereditary right.
2. Representation on the basis of socially independent grouping ("Standische Reprasentation"). This would be a socially privileged group asserting the right to bind others.
3. Instructed representation.
4. Free representation.

Weber argues that the first three forms were known in early times.[10] (We can note independently that in essence these parallel traditional forms of monarchy, aristocracy, and democracy and were defended and rationalized largely in this form. That is to say, they were thought of as attributes of the total system, not as a separate process of representation. The Greeks, then, had a representational system but had no word for it.)

What is unique in modern times is the rise of "free representation," the notion of the legislator exercising judgment. Weber attributes this to the influence of the secularized modernizing and centralizing monarch anxious to destroy the vestiges of feudalistic traditions. To maximize his own power, the king encouraged legislators to think of themselves as free from the restrictions of local control and established custom.

[10] Max Weber, *The Theory of Social and Economic Organization*, ed. Talcott Parsons (New York: Oxford University Press, 1947), pp. 416–17.

By encouraging free judgment by legislators, it would appear that the king effectively established a rival that was, in time, to subdue him. This was early recognized by many monarchs whose attitudes toward representative institutions were rather ambivalent. But the need for flexible policy to replace more frozen processes was overwhelming—at least so I extrapolate Weber's argument—so that the growth of centralized monarchies immediately precedes, and is virtually a prerequisite for, representative structures composed of free agents presuming to use their own judgment of public welfare as the basis of their vote. In England, for example, the king seems to have created Parliament as a device to get consent for taxation.[11] Service in Parliament was an imposed burden by which bad news was conveyed back to localities.[12]

Since modern secular states of the type Weber regards as prerequisite to "free representation" are themselves byproducts of the strong monarchies of the seventeenth century and beyond, it is of course logical that theories of uninstructed representation should date from the same era. This is also the era of the genesis of the bureaucratic state, as Weber notes:

> Everywhere the development of the modern state is initiated through the action of the prince. He paves the way for the expropriation of the autonomous and "private" bearers of executive power who stand beside him, of those who in their own right possess the means of administration, warfare, and financial organiza- tion, as well as politically usable goods of all sorts. The whole process is a complete parallel to the development of the capitalist enterprise through gradual expropriation of the independent producers. In the end, the modern state controls the total means of political organization, which actually come together under a single head.[13]

Weber's explanation also helps account for the absence of any prior notion of bureaucratic representation, inasmuch as the analogy requires some antecedent notion of legislative representativeness. It is highly unlikely that such a concept would come first in the administrative sphere, where the easier concept of employee or agent predominates. Indeed, the obvious rationaliza- tion that control is exercised by someone, both in selection (hiring and firing) and in supervision of policy seems to obviate the need for any further explanation. His Majesty's postman or clerk seems no more a matter for popular control or concern than His Majesty's butler or ship captain. And when autocratic rule gave way to more pluralistic control, the same picture of the relationship prevailed. The bureaucracy was seen as an instrument under

---

[11] See M. J. Clarke, *Medieval Representation and Consent* (New York: Longmans, Green, 1936).

[12] Albert Beebe White, *Self Government at the King's Command* (Minneapolis: University of Minnesota Press, 1933), pp. 128–29.

[13] H. H. Gerth and C. W. Mills, eds., *From Max Weber* (New York: Oxford University Press, 1958), p. 82.

parliamentary control effectuated through ministerial responsibility (or perhaps more accurately as under ministerial control with accountability to parliament).


## V. THE MODERN UBIQUITY OF BUREAUCRACY

We have already noticed that institutions under the same names evolve over time and may be transformed. Bureaucracies today are not only larger and more complex; the development of various techniques of management control, computer memory banks, and accounting systems are all part of what Kenneth Boulding calls the organizational revolution.[14] Government has not merely been affected by this—it has, particularly in wartime and crisis, led the way.

The real history of modern government is the rise of efficient and flexible bureaucracies. Kenneth Davis wrote:

> Marx failed to foresee that government could protect against the abuses of free enterprise, that government could intervene to prevent extreme maldistribution. Marx failed to foresee the potentialities of taxing and spending to provide for the general welfare. Marx failed to foresee the modern regulatory agency.[15]

Davis's argument was parochially American, and limited to the proposition that the welfare state—neither capitalist nor socialist—was made possible by the managerial revolution in technique, training, and skill. But that revolution has also made possible giant conglomerates and international affiliates and highly developed structures.

And the further complement of Davis's argument is that, for Communist regimes as well, Marx's analysis underestimated the force of bureaucracy. This position is most clearly articulated in the writings of Milovan Djilas, especially his *The New Class*.[16] Djilas suggests the Marxist ideal of a classless society is constantly threatened by the emergence of a bureaucracy which is in essence a class combining both the Marxist characteristic of control of the means of production with political control. Djilas's position was important more for the authoritativeness of the writer than for the originality of thought involved. (William Graham Sumner used to tell his classes in the latter part of the nineteenth century, "Gentlemen, if the time ever comes when this country is run by a committee, I have one bit of advice for you: Get on the committee." More to the point, similar espousals by James Burnham—to be

---

[14] Kenneth Boulding, *The Organizational Revolution* (New York: Harper, 1953).
[15] Kenneth Davis in Walter Gellhorn, *Individual Freedom and Government Restraint* (Baton Rouge: Louisiana State University Press, 1956), p. 54.
[16] Milovan Djilas, *The New Class* (New York: Praeger, 1957).

discussed shortly—had preceded Djilas's efforts.) But Djilas's prominence and directness of expression have made his views extensively known.

Since Djilas's book was published, his notions have had some pronounced confirmation from surprising sources. The Russians have modified Marxist theory to suggest party leadership can constitute a "stratum" (not, of course, a class, which in Marxist terms revolves around ownership) remote from the people. The Yugoslav and the aborted Czechoslovakian party efforts to democratize and humanize Marx (in part by emphasizing his earlier writings) reflect the same concern with the routinization of human relations and the dominance of bureaucracy. Perversely enough, Maoist cultural revolutionary efforts, seemingly the antithesis of Titoism, are predicated upon the same distrust of the bureaucrat, though the Maoists find the solution in ruthless voluntarism—man can be transformed by sheer assertion—rather than in a sense of civility and respectful comradeship.

## VI.  THE MODERN DISTRUST OF BUREAUCRACY

It is instructive to see, then, that democrats and various Communists all share distrust for the phenomenon of increasing bureaucratization in their midst. Indeed, as S. N. Eisenstadt points out, all modern ideologies are at least ambivalent, if not actually hostile, toward this seemingly universal development.[17] The most important development in human affairs in this century has thus occurred without the sanction of legitimacy from *any* of the dominant social viewpoints prevailing today.

It is also instructive to note that this ambivalence is reflected in criticisms of at least three separate roles or types under this rubric of bureaucratization. We shall now discuss each of these in turn.

### The Political Power Elite

It is by no means clear that Djilas (or even Mao) is primarily concerned with lower-order or middle management. Particularly where legislators are mere fronts, political party processes become a substitute forum for political demonstration of choice—but also then contribute to rigidity. Djilas's criticisms apply primarily to the group controlling the Communist parties, and largely parallel Robert Michels's analysis of such organs.[18] In a sense, then, Djilas is not criticizing, as he thinks, functionaries of government service but rather, as he sometimes suggests, the power of decision-makers who

---

[17] S. N. Eisenstadt, *Essays on Comparative Institutions* (New York: John Wiley, 1965), p. 180.

[18] Michels, *Political Parties: A Sociological Study of Oligarchical Tendencies of Modern Democracies* (New York: Free Press, 1911, 1962).

comprehensively control at one time economic decisions, political power, and the shaping of opinion. That these happen to be party functionaries is the key, not that they occupy bureaucratic positions. Djilas suggested, "The party makes the class but the class grows as a result and uses the party as a basis. The class grows stronger while the party grows weaker." [19] As T. B. Bottomore points out, the party has hardly withered or weakened to any appreciable extent, or in any irrevocable or clear direction.[20] Certainly, the data from Brzezinski and Huntington given in Table 2.1 reflect something different. The invasion of Czechoslovakia makes sense only in party (possibly also in army) terms, but no other major groups seem to have been consulted, nor were they likely to approve.

**TABLE 2.1    Primary Institutional Connection of Top Soviet Leaders: Party Presidium and Secretariat Combined**

|  | Stalin 1949 (N = 15) | Malenkov 1953 (N = 18) | Bulganin-Khrushchev 1956 (N = 21) | Khrushchev 1962 (N = 21) |
|---|---|---|---|---|
| Professional apparatchik | 54% | 61% | 67% | 81% |
| (Ideologue) | (7%) | (11%) | (14%) | (20%) |
| State bureaucracy | 33% | 28% | 23% | 19% |
| (Industrial) | (20%) | (17%) | (14%) | (5%) |
| Police and Military | 13% | 11% | 9% | — |
| Total | 100% | 100% | 100% | 100% |

Source: Zbigniew Brzezinski and Samuel P. Huntington, "Cincinnatus and the Apparatchik," in *World Politics*, Vol. XVI, copyright © 1963 by Princeton University Press, p. 71.

## The Technocrats or Experts

The argument of James Burnham's *Managerial Revolution*[21] echoes the views of Thorstein Veblen's *Engineer and the Profit System*, or, even more distant, those of St. Simon. That extraordinary thinker was a progenitor of many ideologies. E. H. Carr calls him the father of Marxism, a relationship suggested by his technocratic program "to each according to his ability, to each ability according to its results." St. Simon extolled only the worker, the achiever, and had nothing but contempt for the clerks and their epitomiza-

---

[19] Djilas, *The New Class*, p. 40.
[20] T. B. Bottomore, *Elites and Society* (New York: Basic Books, 1964), pp. 78–79.
[21] James Burnham, *Managerial Revolution* (New York: John Day, 1941).

tion in the rulers, the clergy, and the nobility. In a celebrated passage, he contrasted the possible disappearance of fifty rulers with no real loss to society with the tragic paralysis of the loss of fifty leading physicists and chemists. The valuable people to him were "the scientists, artists, and artisans, the only men whose work is a positive utility to society and cost it practically nothing, who are kept down by the princes and other rulers, who are simply more or less incapable bureaucrats." [22]

Burnham is rather more eclectic. He saw the New Dealers, for example, as technocrats, a description hardly apt for any of its leading figures—Roosevelt, Wallace, Ickes, Perkins, Hopkins—who diluted loosely articulated ideology with infusions of political pragmatism, but had virtually no technical training or competence. In terms of currently prevailing standards of management, they would be almost classic generalists with little mastery of technical skills to apply to their problems. Similarly, Burnham in 1941 saw the civil service—not the party and the specialists in violence—as controlling Nazi Germany; this was an extremely inept analysis.

But Burnham's main theme is that engineers control key operations in society and that owners are increasingly remote and uninformed. Control means eventual ownership, the supplanting of those not able to protect their legal relationship by technical and practical means.[23] He sees conflict between those who do, and those who merely own or manage by prerogative. The experts, the engineers, are coming into their own, more often bloodlessly than not, as a separation of ownership and practical control continues. Burnham saw the United States, Fascist Italy, and Communist Russia as differing forms of the same system of progressively developing technocratic control.

The difficulty is simply that the analysis and prophecy seems shortsighted, if not muddle-headed, both from the viewpoint of when it was written and from our vantage point three decades later. As Gerth and Mills pointed out, at the time of Burnham's work the functionary or technocrat was neither pugnacious nor assertive, nor hardly likely to discard legal control. Rather he is by nature inclined to accept direction and control.[24] Technocrats seem even less likely to control matters in an age of "human administration" which emphasizes a specialist training in generalism.

### The Semispecialist Interpreter and Intermediary

It is rather the man who can interpret and deal with technicians who

---

[22] Quoted in Samuel Krislov, *The Negro in Federal Employment* (Minneapolis: University of Minnesota Press, 1967), p. 52.

[23] Burnham, *Managerial Revolution*, pp. 84–87.

[24] Gerth and Mills, "A Marx for the Managers," reprinted in C. Wright Mills, *Power, Politics and the People* (New York: Oxford University Press, 1963), pp. 53–76.

looms as powerful. Thus, in the Soviet Union, Aleksei Kosygin comes closest to personifying Burnham's notion; but he is more properly described as a party man who dealt with industry. Figures, such as Mikhail Pervukhian, whose careers were predominantly technical, do not seem to have had great longevity. The go-between is above all rational and goal-directed. As Mosca points out, he is organized and selected to further set goals. He accepts and by and large requires the external setting of goals. His triumph is that of the technical semispecialist whose formation-absorption skills allow him to transfer from structure to structure. A Robert MacNamara who goes from business college teaching to automobile manufacturing to defense policy to the World Bank personifies this type in many of its strengths and some of its weaknesses as well.

An interesting example of this role and how easily it is confounded is the case of Albert Speer, the man who headed the German economy during most of World War II. His celebrated apologia *Inside the Third Reich* became an American and international best-seller. One of his basic themes was his claim that as a technocrat he was peculiarly vulnerable to Hitler's blandishments. In a brilliant and devastating book review, the British historian Geoffrey Barraclough examined and exploded most of Speer's posturing, especially on this point.[25] Speer was an architect by training with very little knowledge of engineering and science, but just enough to occupy his position in a regime of poorly trained ideologues. With more competence—say had Speer's predecessor remained alive—the war might even have ended differently.

## VII.  THE PROLIFERATION OF ADMINISTRATIVE STRUCTURE

The rise of governmental bureaucracies is largely the history of an increase of middle-range positions, with moderately comfortable salaries and considerable, but not primary, discretion and responsibility. These positions include such functions as fiscal control, legal review, direct government participation in developing entrepreneurship, and the like. The early government employee was typically in the post office or a defense shipyard—a blue-collar worker. As two careful students of governmental employment note:

On the eve of World War I, the British central government was still mainly a government of soldiers and sailors, postal clerks, and tax collectors. The only marked change over two generations was the sizeable staff of industrial workers

---

[25] Albert Speer, *Inside the Third Reich* (New York: Macmillan, 1970), reviewed by Geoffrey Barraclough in the *New York Review of Books*, January 9, 1971, pp. 6–14.

required in the government-owned armament establishments. But regulatory and social service activities still counted for little. By the broadest definition they absorbed not ten percent of the civilian employees of the central government and not more than four percent of the military and civilian staffs together.[26]

Today's model civil servant is a lawyer, an accountant, a master of public administration, a typical member of the "salariat" with professional or semiprofessional attitudes.

This rise is hardly unique to government; much the same pattern is repeated in other sectors of a developing economy. As round-about manufacture replaces simple direct production in the field, a series of supplementary specializations develop. At first glance many seem to have only tangential connections with productivity; yet as the field of visual art illustrates, seemingly remote skills can be marshalled for modern production and distribution purposes.

The growth of such structures at the governmental level betokens a relative loosening of the power of the major, more visible, policy makers. In democratic societies, this involves two shifts, both well known: from legislative to executive control, and from higher-level to middle-level bureaucratic disposal. However, legitimacy and ultimate power remain with the upper echelons. Real showdowns, when they have occurred, have been decisive and work to strengthen the upper echelons' hands. Bureaucracy grows by accretion, not by revolution.

## VIII.  WHY DO BUREAUCRACIES GROW?

Some years ago, an explanation of bureaucratic growth was set forth in terms that have become virtually classic; they are worth summarizing here. The Attorney General's Committee on Administrative Procedure of 1941 suggested a number of reasons for congressional use of such agencies, in spite of an aversion to strengthening another branch of government:

1. The desire to protect the citizen through use of administrative rather than purely presidential officials and therefore to create officers with greater individual discretionary prerogatives.
2. To limit the power of the courts to prevent their use as an agency of administration.
3. The need for a more flexible method of anticipating and preventing unwanted results rather than meting out punishment after the fact.
4. Because of the limitations on effective legislative action: the press of time, the

[26] Moses Abramovitz and Vera F. Eliasberg, *The Growth of Public Employment in Great Britain* (Princeton, N.J.: Princeton University Press, 1957), p. 39.

need for specialized information, and the availability of a specialized staff and procedures to deal with complex problems.

5. The advantage of unified policy through agency procedure rather than through isolated proceedings.

6. The advantages of continuity of attention by a specialized agency with clearly allocated responsibility, over a diffuse allocation to different sources.

7. The need for an organization to dispose of a large volume of business and to provide the necessary records.

The Attorney General's Committee also set forth in often-repeated terms some of the major characteristics of these agencies:

1. Size. "Most administrative agencies are of necessity large organizations." Some agencies have large numbers of personnel; the Veterans Administration, for example, has about 175,000 employees.

2. Specialization. "Administrative agencies specialize in particular tasks, and they include specialists on their staffs." The procedures and style of administration characteristic of such agencies are, in large measure, products of specialization and the resultant habits of mind.

3. Responsibility for results. "An administrative agency is usually charged with accomplishing or attempting to accomplish some end specified in the statute." This means that the agencies cannot take a wholly passive attitude toward the issues which come before them. They are entrusted with developing and carrying out an integrated program of wide scope.

4. Variety of administrative duties. "No single fact is more striking in a review of existing Federal administrative agencies than the variety of the duties which are entrusted to them to perform. . . . This central and inescapable fact makes generalization and description difficult."

The complexity of organization and the specialized technical nature of many of the activities of the regulatory agencies have made them little noticed in popular discussion. In fact their specialization and complexity make them difficult to discuss; their ubiquity becomes another reason they stay unexamined.

## IX.  MODELS OF BUREAUCRATIC GROWTH

We can suggest three patterns of growing bureaucratic power. The above explanations and characteristics describe the first type—the increasing complexity of Western neocapitalist governmental structures.

In the second pattern, Communist structures merge into governmental functions; under capitalism these relationships are handled through private bureaucracies and the market mechanism. The first effect is, of course, to swell the ranks of the public bureaucracy. The second consequence is to make middle-rank officials more important.

As Bertram Gross points out, increases in bureaucratic size have relatively little effect upon the number of top decision-makers.[27] The need for final resolution means little opening at the top. As structures increase in size, the consequence is a steepening or a widening of the hierarchical structure.

Widened                    Steepened

In consequence, the twin issues of bureaucratic size and decisions by less visible officeholders loom large in Communist countries. In country after country—Czechoslovakia, Yugoslavia, China, and Russia itself—large-scale public campaigns on the issue of control of such functionaries have been common.

Since Communist theory since Lenin emphasizes centralized control, the orthodox countries adopt ever-steeper decision structures. As Michael Polanyi argues on philosophical and technical grounds, such a structure encourages autocracy. Information theory suggests that with entropy and general costs of communication such a complex and inflexible system will be relatively inefficient over any long haul.[28]

The third type of modern bureaucracy is that of developing countries. Here clearly the bulging of both governmental service and the middle ranks is also repeated. By and large, in such countries, the lack of free-floating capital has meant that development and entrepreneurship is largely concentrated within the government. New business efforts are crucial to societal growth, and assume awesome significance when the availability of positions exercising skill is considered. Thus, public service here, too, is very important in determining social outcome and in total productive employment. As in Communist countries, the monopolistic concentration of political and economic power lends urgency to the problem of controlling discretion.

Thus, though particulars vary, the problem of growing bureaucratic

[27] See Bertram Gross, *The Managing of Organization: The Administrative Struggle*, (New York: Free Press, 1964).

[28] See the article by Michael Polanyi in Raymond Aron, ed., *World Technology and Human Destiny* (Ann Arbor: University of Michigan Press, 1963), pp. 102–21. An unpublished paper by Theodore Meckstroth applies much the same analysis to a federal system.

power recurs throughout the major types of bureaucratic governmental systems. On a practical level, all try to cope with modern problems through an extension of bureaucracy. On an ideological level, all find it hard to justify or rationalize the phenomenon.

## X. THE DEMOCRATIC DILEMMA

In democratic societies, the issue of bureaucratic power has a peculiar poignancy. Why go through the elaborate razzle-dazzle of elections if the crucial element is the discretion of a bureau chief? More charades are not needed in our society, which is notoriously direct in attitude, but which has more than its share of empty formalism.

Some writers simply place their faith in the facts of legality, in the clear-cut ultimate power of popular government. Charles Hyneman, for example, finds a simple answer, entitling a chapter in his *Bureaucracy in a Democracy* somewhat off-handedly "Solution: Political Supremacy." [29] He thus calls for increased popular control over administration through a clear definition of administrative responsibility. The civil service should act as Congress would have them act. Similarly, those who assume presidential control are generally also stressing popular responsibility though they find the repository of popular will elsewhere. Throughout our history, some have ascribed the highest measure of representability to each of these different organs. Until the Vietnam war, for example, those groups espousing what is called a "liberal ideology" have in this century focused their hopes upon the presidency, while conservatives have come to see Congress as embodying the popular will. This has some ironic, if not perverse, aspects, but both arguments presuppose popular sovereignty, or pretend to.

Those who support a more detached professionalism, who see administrations as having a more creative role, present a differing view of responsibility. Ultimately, they must find some justification for the growing powers of discretion. One quite common assertion is that issues increasingly are scientific or technical, devoid of social significance or political overtones, and therefore are best solved by experts removed from such pressures. As society becomes more complex, problems, it is argued, become less controversial and more scientific. This view had more currency a few decades ago, but experience has diminished its persuasiveness. The claims of urban planners, for instance, have not been matched by performance.

Similarly, in other areas, unchecked expert opinion no longer promises frictionless, pure decision-making. The notion of neutral, professional city managers is now regarded as at least in part a disguised form of resolving that

---

[29] Charles Hyneman, *Bureaucracy in a Democracy* (New York: Harper, 1950), p. 56.

certain issues will not be raised. The recognition that decisions cannot simply be reduced to a net gain or loss analysis is relevant here; it was the hope of the welfare economists, especially those following A. C. Pigou, that they could prove the desirability of specific policies through such cost analyses. In actual operation, they could indeed assign, say, a dollar value to increased medical bills caused by smoke pollution as opposed to costs of installing preventive equipment. But the result was not convincing in close cases; whether a few individuals should risk lung cancer or corporations risk bankruptcy seemed more relevant and more a matter of social views than the cost accounting argument which merely offered one index—and a rather poor one—of social welfare. In short, in both practical and theoretical terms, we have demonstrated in the past few decades a more circumscribed role for the expert than that claimed by extreme believers. His role has been vindicated, to be sure; in public affairs the era of decision by pure intuition, without information, is gone. Exaggerated notions that social decisions can be brought into being by technocratic storks have been replaced by the surer realization that public choices necessarily involve consequences for individuals, consequences that usually include sacrifices as well as gains. Professionalism thus emerges as, at best, only a partial justification for decisions. No matter how objective the decision-maker, consequences are best evaluated subjectively. We come back to Aristotle: the humble taster is as good a judge of the meal as the gourmet cook.

## XI.   LEGITIMIZING THE AMERICAN BUREAUCRATIC STATE

In the face of these developments, some writers have ventured a more direct defense. "The rich diversity that makes up the United States is better represented in its civil service than anywhere else," notes Norton Long; the argument is clear-cut. Because of its representative nature, the bureaucracy need not be apologetic in exercise of its authority. It shares legitimacy with—to take the American example—the presidency and Congress. It may in consequence share in authority and in the assumption of responsibility.

> Responsibility is a product of responsible institutions; and with all their deficiencies—which are many indeed—the departments of administration come closer than any other organs of government to achieving responsible behavior by virtue of the breadth and depth of their consideration of the relevant facts and because of the representative character of their personnel. As continuing organizations, they can learn from their mistakes. They can even make their mistakes meaningful. That is, they can make explicit to themselves the hypotheses on which they act and so make failure itself a source of knowledge. In

however limited a form, these agencies are organized to make self-corrective behavior possible.[30]

The notion that the bureaucracy is in fact representative is advanced in two separate ways: (1) it is seen as such in composition and in the manner of its selection; (2) it is judged in terms of substantive product, and the quality of its decisions is evaluated in the light of their accord with what is assumed to be public opinion. The two arguments are intertwined, and it is clear that results alone would not justify the defense without certain assumptions about the validity of the first claim. Davidson suggests the theme well: "Analytically, the test of representation is whether, in public policy-making, the demands or interests of every relevant definable public have been effectively articulated." [31] However, weaknesses in each of the arguments often go unnoticed, at least in part, because evidence for one is confused with evidence for the other.

The representativeness of the American bureaucracy can be asserted in simple, factual terms. A broad range of talents, types, and social and ethnic backgrounds is to be found in the operative portions of government. Given these facts, the method of selection is subordinated to results. Objective, nondiscriminatory testing can, it is argued, perform selection and retain legitimate representational aspects; we can regard the Athenian selection by lottery as a form of such "objective" selection in much the same manner.

Nor is the purely electoral process free from chance or from designed-in elements involving distortion of popular will. Gerrymandering and less overt systematic efforts to pervert electoral systems are omnipresent; a leading study finds a universal bias in election systems always favoring the largest party in two-party systems, and even more so in multiple-party systems.[32] There are good functional reasons for this; election systems are designed to provide viable governments as well as mirror opinion. Insofar as it succeeds in subtly—or even openly—beefing up the majority, an electoral system necessarily departs from puristic representativeness. When a small popular majority produces a larger legislative majority—or complete control of the executive—the governmental advantages seem to outweigh the costs of distortion. However, other modifications of popular will may be less subtle, less justifiable, less based on popular choice, and yet probably inevitable. The committee structure of Congress necessarily entrusts policies to a substructure which must seriously distort broad opinion. Specialization of committees means precisely that those most involved in an issue are most decisive. Committee assignment is a personal matter, not, except indirectly, a product

[30] Norton Long, *The Polity* (Chicago: Rand McNally, 1962), p. 73.

[31] Davidson, "Congress and the Executive: The Race for Representation," p. 366.

[32] Douglas W. Rae, *The Political Consequences of Electoral Laws* (New Haven, Conn.: Yale University Press, 1967, 1971).

of constituency characteristics, and there is no particular notion of representation of the total public on any individual committee. Yet for all practical
purposes a committee may be the decisive force over an entire domain of
policy. The notorious seniority system and the vagaries of career routes also
mean that power is exercised in random ways unrelated to any aspect of
public choice.

Similarly, the institutionalization of the Presidency makes it difficult to
see any straightforward public choice in the exercise of executive power. The
White House staff and generally the Executive Office of the President are
composed of people whose selection partakes perhaps even less of public
choice than overtly civil service positions. At least the rules for the selection of
the latter have some public and democratic character. But it would be a
useless exercise in sophistry to try to indicate where the popularly chosen,
legitimate, representative Presidency ends, and the massive, bureaucratic,
nonrepresentative Administrative branch begins. The argument here is not
merely that other branches are not as clearly representative as commonly
thought. Rather, it is that direct popular choice is not the only test of
representativeness and indeed may not be the determining one.

If we accept that fundamental argument, the rest follows easily. In social
composition the federal bureaucracy ranges more widely than any small
popularly elected group could. From this, it is urged we must look at results,
at what is done:

> Responsible behavior in the sense of sensitivity to long-range and broad
> considerations, the totality of interests affected, and the utilization of expert
> knowledge by procedures that ensure a systematic collection and analysis of
> relevant facts, is more characteristic of the executive than of Congress. Despite
> the exceptions, and there are many, this kind of responsible behavior is more
> expected, more politically feasible, and more frequently practiced in the
> administrative branch. The bureaucracy headed by the presidency is both
> compelled and encouraged to respond to, and even to assist in the development
> of broad publics . . . , but broad publics seldom emanate from the organization
> and the geographic concentration necessary for effectiveness in the congressional
> committee process.[33]

On the whole, the argument that "representativeness" is primarily a
product remains novel to us. It seems to minimize the difference between
democratic and nondemocratic systems by depreciating elections. But this
itself is perhaps to be expected in an era in which elections have proven a
useful tool of totalitarians, who have found in the popular plebescite mixed
with a dash of terror an unrivaled instrument of popular control, mobiliza-
tion of opinion, and symbol of legitimacy, all obtainable at minimum risk to
authority. Long finds elections wanting even in our system:

[33] Long, *The Polity*, p. 68.

To the modern student of government, Aristotle's characterization of an election as an oligarchical device always comes somewhat as a shock. Nonetheless, its implications for representative democracy are significant. If one were to set forth in law the facts of life of the American Congress, it would appear that, to be eligible, overwhelmingly a candidate had first to be in the upper upper-income bracket or second, either personally or through his associates, to be able to command substantial sums of money. Expressed as custom, such conditions are passed over save for the carping criticism of Marxists; yet if they were expressed in law, they would clearly characterize our constitution as oligarchic.[34]

If we accept the argument about the representativeness of the American bureaucracy, then we must also accept it as applying to others as well. Taking Kingsley and Long as formulated, we would also have the possibility of developing criteria by which to judge such structures. In short, Long's arguments justifying bureaucratic authority can just as well be invoked as standards of judgment à la Kingsley.

> As it operates in the civil service, the recruitment process brings into federal employment and positions of national power, persons whose previous affiliations, training, and background cause them to conceive of themselves as representing constituencies that are relatively uninfluential in Congress. These constituencies, like that of the presidency, are in the aggregate numerically very large; and in speaking for them as self-appointed, or frequently actually appointed, representatives, the bureaucrats fill in the deficiencies of the process of representation in the legislature. The importance of this representation lies not only in offsetting such defects as rural overrepresentation, the self-contained district, and other vagaries of our system of nominations that leave many without a voice, but in the qualitative representation of science, the professions, the institutions of learning, and the conscience of society as it is expressed in churches, civil liberties groups, and a host of others.[35]

In this respect, as in many others, Long follows Mosca who in a celebrated passage derided elections:

> The truth is that the representative *has himself elected* by the voters, and, if that phrase should seem too inflexible and too harsh to fit some cases, we might qualify it by saying that *his friends have him elected.* In elections, as in all other manifestations of social life, those who have the will and, especially, the moral, intellectual and material *means* to force their will upon others take the lead over the others and command them.[36]

While elections do provide some democratic protection involving "the

---

[34] Long, *The Polity*, p. 69.
[35] Long, *The Polity*, p. 70.
[36] Mosca, *The Ruling Class*, p. 154.

circulation of elites," "the real juridical safeguard in representative government is the public discussion that takes place within representative assemblies." [37] But such discussion is, in parliament after parliament, on the decline
and legislatures are on the defensive. The modern representative system still
reflects a delicate balance between bureaucratic and legislative power. The
interaction of the two may or may not prove an adequate substitute for close
surveillance by the popular branches of government. In any event, it is clear
that, increasingly, effective and informed legislative debate is dependent
upon intrabureaucratic disagreement and the consequent leaking of information to the legislature.

It is to these questions that the rest of this volume is addressed. To what
extent and in what sense can bureaucracies be representative? Should they be
so? What are the patterns prevailing in modern bureaucracies? What do
differences in composition signify?

The answers to these and related questions touch upon a surprising
range of significant social and economic questions. The failure of a white,
middle-class administered poverty program to stir up much except controversy is related to its social bearing. In New York City an educational crisis is
best understood as a conflict of values between a rabidly suspicious Black
community and a bureaucracy—largely Jewish—which finds departures
from its own sense of academic priorities personally threatening. In Nigeria a
civil war emerged from the fantastic success of the Ibos in securing
bureaucratic power over other tribes through personal efficiency—an
efficiency which could only be dealt with by a massacre of the Ibos. Fear of
similar conflict reluctantly led the Tunku, Abdul Rahmin, premier of the
Malaysian states, to suggest dismemberment of the Union so that the
energetically successful Chinese concentrated in Singapore would not arouse
the animosity of his compatriots. In short, throughout the world, bureaucracy
is the blood, bone, and sinews of political power. Its composition dictates and
reflects policy. And that composition cries out for study.

## XII.  CONCLUSION AND SUMMARY

The term "representative" has itself evolved through history. Its current
sense of agent-trustee in legislative circles is itself a recent development. Until
the modern extensive political state began to develop in the late seventeenth
century there was little need for the formal device of representation or its
legitimation; only in the past century has it emerged as the characteristic
principle undergirding and providing legitimacy for the modern state.

Bureaucracies are the late bloomers of modern political structure. They

---

[37] Mosca, *The Ruling Class*, p. 157.

grew silently, inexorably in the underbrush—seldom noticed, little analyzed. Convenience and necessity, not ideology and legitimacy, are their life-blood; they are not loved and respected, but rather tolerated and depended on.

All the great forms of the modern state join in excoriating bureaucracy and then proceed to build and expand it. For each of these three societal types there are ideological contradictions inherent in these expanding structures. The problem for mass middle-class democracies of the American type is perhaps the greatest, and ideologists have attempted to justify such structures at some length, and in fairly convincing style.

# 3

# *Why Bureaucracies Can Never Be Fully Representative*

## I. INTRODUCTION

Having sketched a history of the concept of representative bureaucracy and having traced the emergence of demands for it, we are now ready to consider its validity. This chapter will consider its limitations, and Chapter 4 will consider its advantages and potential.

One method of considering an argument is to examine a generalized extreme form of the case—either real or imaginary. We will do this in the following section. The ideal extreme case can often illuminate situations more satisfactorily than the more blurred interaction of cause and effect involved in more typical and eclectic cases.

## II. GOVERNMENT BY SAMPLING: A TEST CASE

The extreme case in the application of notions of representation has long been recognized as that of ancient Athens. The Athenian citizens refused, it is said, to delegate their powers except under dire necessity. To maintain maximum control they presumably undertook direct legislation in open, mass meetings. To permit continuity, the establishment of an agenda for the popular assembly, and similar housekeeping functions, they were forced to establish a council but kept it strictly controlled by making it an extremely large and cumbersome unit—about 1,000 persons. Even more significantly they minimized its importance and stature by selecting its members by lot.[1] Thus every Athenian citizen was not only eligible for service but was potentially as eligible in fact, as well as in law, as any other citizen. Public service was thus every man's right, an Athenian birthright, which apparently required no special qualification.

Lottery was seen as a logical extension of democracy as a system of government; if the people generally and not the aristocracy were to rule the people, then not merely the best were to serve. Aristotle found the lottery most conducive to democracy. Although election by all of all was still a means consistent with democracy: "In the appointment of magistrates, for example, the use of the lot is regarded as democratic and the use of the vote as oligarchical." [2] And while the lot was used for nondemocratic purposes in a few instances, it was employed not only in Athens but also in other Greek and Italian city-states, mostly under populist regimes. The additional effect, beyond dispersal of the right to office, was to limit the power of the officeholder. No mandate or other strong endorsement was given the functionary. Limits upon years of service further decreased the authority and power of officeholders because rotation in office insured weak administration. To further democratic control as well as to permit duties to be performed under conditions of extreme turnover, each office was routinized and made as simple in its execution as possible. Close accounting and examination of the conduct of office was required at the expiration of the term of office and the possibility of severe punishment at the hands of the popular assembly faced those officers whose conduct the examiners assessed as faulty.

Such at least was the ideal of Athenian democracy as interpreted by Western historians.[3] It avoided discretionary power by routinized subdivision of authority; the accretion of power by rotation in office and limits upon successive terms; and the trappings of power by lack of qualification for office and the use of the vagaries of fate through a lottery.

But these claims are overblown. From the beginning it is clear the system

---

[1] George Thomson suggests the word "lot" for property originates in a Greek custom of distributing land through chance. See Thomson, *Studies in Ancient Greek Society,* Vol. I (New York: International Publishing, 1949), p. 327.

[2] Aristotle, *Politics,* E. Barker, trans. (New York: Oxford University Press, 1962), p. 177.

[3] See esp. James Wycliffe Headlam, *Election by Lot in Athens,* 2nd ed. rev. by D. C. MacGregor (Cambridge, Eng.: Cambridge University Press, 1933). Headlam's lavish claims for lotteries have had to be modified by later historians.

deviated from strict lottery and further deviations were introduced over time. Even putting aside the marked, and often discussed, lack of genuine democracy due to large-scale disenfranchisement of slaves, women, and non-Athenians, discrepancies existed. These deviations had specific justifications, and further modifications were made in much the same directions, so much so that A. H. M. Jones's authoritative *Athenian Democracy* characterizes the system as basically aristocratic.[4] Specifically, it deviated from abstract theory in that:

1. From the beginning, nominations were made at a meeting of the demes (a loose tribelike grouping) from a number exceeding the positions open for that deme. It would appear that the ensuing lottery was not a free-for-all. The nominees from each deme were merely brought to a central point for a deme-by-deme lottery. Selection from this point seems to have been almost strictly by deme; the variation from strict equality of deme representation is so small that it could not have occurred by chance. Rather, it would appear deviations were permitted if less than the required number of candidates emerged or if some special occasion suggested that one deme nominate a member of another, for example, if, in time of crisis, several military leaders happened to be from one deme.[5]

In short, the lottery was not random but *stratified* to assure *representation* of each deme. This representation had in it certain elements of convenience, for a place and time to gather suggestions were afforded by the annual meetings of the demes. It is also probable that compliance was a factor; these same meetings were intimately involved in tax collections and tax allocation. Representation of each deme, not abstract randomness, was useful and recognized in the system.[6]

2. The names forwarded to the lottery, it seems, were clearly not randomly chosen. Volunteers were sought and selection made from them if there was an excess. (Evidence for this includes explicit comment by Greek playwrights and other commentators.) More empirically, the presence on the rolls of large numbers of relatives, particularly fathers and sons, far exceeds any reasonable coincidence. The inference is that they volunteered to serve or actively mobilized support.[7] Zimmern, for example, assumes an election in each deme preceded the lottery which selected from such eligibles.[8] In most instances the rate of pay for office was not sufficient to support those lacking supplementary funds. The dangers attendant to public service were not

---

[4] A. H. M. Jones, *Athenian Democracy* (Oxford: B. Blackwell, 1957), pp. 48–49.

[5] Alfred Zimmern, *The Greek Commonwealth* (Oxford: Oxford University Press, paperback ed., 1961), pp. 155–56.

[6] Headlam, *Election by Lot in Athens*, pp. 187–88. See also J. A. O. Larsen, *Representative Government in Greek and Roman History* (Berkeley: University of California Press, 1955).

[7] See MacGregor's critique of Headlam in *Elections by Lot in Athens*, p. 192.

[8] Zimmern, *The Greek Commonwealth*, p. 162.

theoretical. Death, banishment, and fines for former officials came often with shifts in political opinion. Volunteers had to be able to afford public service, and to value it above obvious costs. At least some positions at various times went begging, and it seems clear that generally in most demes any volunteer was likely to have his name forwarded for the final lottery.[9] Thus, intensity of interest, willingness to assume the office, and ability to serve given the fiscal terms were all modifiers of strict proportionality.

3. In many instances *technical qualifications for office* had to be introduced. This was particularly true of accounting and other fiscal positions. These were minimized by the process of subdividing responsibilities, but some restriction of eligibility was prescribed.[10]

4. Requirements for reeligibility to continue serving in the *crucial offices*, particularly the military office of general, were drastically different. Here, also, where military efficiency was at stake, the usual processes of selection were not sufficient. While it is not clear how wide the scope of the general responsibility actually was, it is clear that it was not insignificant.

5. Corruption at the level of the demes and even in the lottery process ultimately led to its abandonment. *Ease of selection and accountability* for the results thus appear as yet another limit upon microreproduction of societal composition.

6. A. H. M. Jones points out that all our descriptions and defenses of Athenian democracy were written by its enemies, or have been distilled from dry records. Not a single exposition of the ideology of this government remains from its proponents. We must, therefore, approach these matters with a sense of diffidence and—quite properly—with some extra sympathy for the absent defendant in an ex parte proceeding.

Nonetheless, Socrates' criticism as quoted by Xenephon echoes through the ages: "It was silly that the rulers of the city should be appointed by lot when no one would be willing to employ a pilot or a carpenter or a flutist chosen by lot." [11] Thus it would appear that the *process of selection should also have plausibility and impart legitimacy*. As far as we can tell the Greeks did not accept the full implication of absolute equality. Pericles indeed argues merely for service in public life "not as a matter of privilege but in recognition of merit; on the other hand, anyone who can benefit the city is not debarred by poverty or by the obscurity of his position." [12] Plato observes in the *Menexenus*, "In truth, it is an aristocracy with the approval of the majority. We have always had kings; sometimes they were hereditary, sometimes elective." [13] In short, Athenians seem to have been unable to accept sheer randomness, either conceptually or in practice, as a proper means of choosing leaders.

[9] For Jones's explicit conclusion to this effect see Jones, *Athenian Democracy*, p. 106.
[10] Jones, *Athenian Democracy*, pp. 101, 103–4.
[11] Quoted in Jones, *Athenian Democracy*, p. 41.
[12] See Thucydides, *The Peloponnesian War*, II, 37, 1.
[13] See Plato, *Menexenus*, 238cd.

We have dealt with this example in detail because it illustrates more general processes. The Athenian democracy, far from contradicting findings like those of R. Michels and G. Mosca on the power of leadership, tends to confirm them. Governmental bureaucracies emerge then as sharing certain characteristics with others—and some unique ones as well—which keep them from representativeness. The Athenian example, like Mao's cultural revolution, constituted an ambitious attempt to overcome the facts of nature. Like its modern analogue it was something less than a total vindication.

## III.  SOME BASIC DISTINCTIONS

"The very rich are different from you and me," Fitzgerald, the supracaninophile,[14] whimpered. "Yes," Hemingway assented, "they have more money." In the same way government bureaucracies are different from simpler aggregations. They are more politicized, more public, and must be legitimized on a basis more ideological and more open to discussion and bargaining.

The justifications for the rise and fall of government units are also different. Profit and loss are relatively meaningless terms, as proved in the periodic juggling with the federal budget (as with loans and repayments from and to Federal Home Loan banks by the Treasury just before and after June 30). Since the banks' transactions are not part of the operating budget—though they are government agencies—a temporary infusion of cash appears while the debt does not appear on that particular budget.[15] Such sleight of hand is of course available to some extent in private transactions. Yet the government's range is sufficiently unlimited to suggest the applicability of Hegel's maxim that differences of degree ultimately become differences in kind.

The chief limit on governmental growth or diminution is not in essence its normal economic activity or consumer interest. It is rather a side product—namely, its ability to produce revenue—that is the determinant. This in turn involves the product of third parties, whose activity is catalyzed rather than controlled by government, and the government's ability to extract its nominal exactions. On the other hand, if it is willing to resort to the printing press and its citizenry will accept its paper money, it can tax it another way.

On the other hand, demand for services is also rather independent of revenue. The movement to the suburbs created demands for streets, lighting, and new schools, all of which contributed to ultimate prosperity but certainly

[14] "A lover of the upper-dog," as distinguished from today's infracaninophiles.
[15] See the *New York Times,* June 26, 1969, p. 55.

yielded little local revenue. The depression required greater governmental expenditure, and indeed local governments helped contribute to the depression by acting reflexively rather than countercyclically. The federal government was forced to still additional expenditures. Revenue may be least when the need is sorest.

Actions and officeholding are subject to a cruder scrutiny and control. Appearances, fads, and irrational public fetishes may be more important than any more durable tests of efficiency.

All of these may create constraints that select and limit participation to persons willing to operate within them. Factors of personality and concepts of public service involve special requirements for recruitment of public officials.

## IV.  LIMITS ON REPRESENTATIVENESS: SKILLS

Governmental bureaucracies are, even more than most, paper empires built upon the memo, the official budget, and the copies for everyone's files. Their appetite for clerical help is unbounded and their need for expert and technical skills is only a little more controlled. In the United States and the United Kingdom in the nineteenth century the preponderance of postal services (and shipyards and armament works) in the government employment picture meant that the public service once had a strong base of unskilled or craft workers.[16] The decline of direct government manufacture of war materials has also been accompanied by a relative standstill in the manpower of the post office. To be sure government buildings still have to be cleaned by janitors and enterprises like TVA require blue-collar workers; even the administering of social security programs requires a base of employees whose clerical tasks involve skills so minimal that they make any white-collar classification questionable in the extreme. But the typical contemporary governmental agency must include the independent regulatory agencies whose functions are carried out by a small group of highly specialized experts and virtually no staff of lesser-skilled individuals. Structures such as NASA with over 35,000 employees or the AEC with 7,500 are remarkably skewed institutions in terms of their high percentages of professional employees. In the main group of federal employees, these differences are consistently present, though not as dramatically as in the two bureaucracies just mentioned. A sampling of the *employed* public as contrasted with a similar sample of federal employees in 1960 confirmed this generally (Table 3.1). Had the comparison been made with the total labor force, the difference would, of course, have been more pronounced.

[16] Moses Abramovitz and Vera F. Eliasberg, *The Growth of Public Employment in Great Britain* (Princeton, N.J.: Princeton University Press, 1957), p. 30.

**TABLE 3.1    Education, Occupation, and Income Among General Federal Employees and the General Employed Public**

| Characteristics | General Federal Employees (N = 948) | General Employed Public | | |
|---|---|---|---|---|
| | | Total (1,142) | Excluding Farm (1,056) | Excluding Self-Employed (924) |
| Education: | | | | |
| High school not completed | 24% | 29% | 27% | 29% |
| High school completed | 39 | 45 | 46 | 46 |
| Some college | 18 | 11 | 11 | 10 |
| College graduate | 14 | 13 | 13 | 12 |
| Other* | 5 | 3 | 3 | 3 |
| Occupation: | | | | |
| Professional, technical, and kindred workers | 18 | 12 | 13 | 13 |
| Farmers and farm managers | 0 | 7 | 0 | 1 |
| Managers, officials, and proprietors | 9 | 14 | 16 | 8 |
| Clerical and kindred workers | 40 | 10 | 11 | 12 |
| Sales workers | ** | 6 | 7 | 6 |
| Craftsmen, foreman, and kindred workers | 19 | 16 | 18 | 19 |
| Operatives and kindred workers | 6 | 22 | 24 | 26 |
| Service workers, except private household | 4 | 6 | 7 | 7 |
| Laborers, except farm and mine | 3 | 4 | 4 | 4 |
| Others | 1 | 2 | 1 | 4 |
| Occupational Income: | | | | |
| Under $3,000 | 1 | 19 | 18 | 22 |
| $3,000–4,999 | 31 | 36 | 37 | 42 |
| $5,000–6,999 | 47 | 27 | 28 | 30 |
| $7,000–9,999 | 13 | 9 | 10 | 3 |
| $10,000–14,999 | 7 | 4 | 4 | 3 |
| $15,000 and over | ** | 4 | 4 | 1 |
| Median Occupational Income*** | $5,500 | $4,700 | $4,700 | $4,600 |
| Median Family Income*** | $7,200 | $5,500 | $5,500 | $5,200 |

*Includes categories such as trade school, nursing, etc., which could not safely be allocated to one of the preceding categories.*
** *Less than 1 percent.*
*** *Rounded to nearest $100.*

Source: Milton C. Cummings, Jr., M. Kent Jennings, and Franklin P. Kilpatrick, "Federal and Non-Federal Employees: A Comparative Social-Occupational Analysis," *Public Administration Review*, XXVII, Dec. 1967, p. 397.

While the largest difference (in the clerical category) is inflated by inclusion of postal workers including mail carriers as "clerical," even adjustment for this would leave the government force more heavily endowed with professional, skilled, and above all clerical workers than the general force. This is also the conclusion of other studies.[17]

The need for training is impressively borne out by the Australian experience. This egalitarian society frowned upon university degrees, and established a "closed bureaucracy" with initial recruitment at age 16, with promotion from within for the administrative class. University degrees were required only for doctors, lawyers, and engineers, and university recruitment was deliberately eschewed for other posts. Limited recruitment of graduates was finally achieved in the 1930s and then expanded, reaching a legally permitted level of 10 percent per annum after World War II. Yet a recent study of 326 senior public servants found 56 percent had university degrees—about a third through part-time education while in service.[18]

Since government service requires skills different from those needed by society as a whole, it cannot reproduce a microcosm of the society. It will of necessity be middle-class in skills and function. Lenin's notion that any worker who learned to add and multiply could become a plant manager has proven a particularly quixotic hope, one based upon total misunderstanding of the difficulties involved. Chester Barnard has argued that introduction of a technological innovation usually requires managerial genius at least as great as that of the original invention.[19] Barnett's anthropological definition of innovation—a recombination of known elements in an unpredicted way—if accepted, would tend to substantiate that view.[20] It is clear that managerial functions are not routine and that not "just anyone" can easily be thrust into a manager's job. On the contrary, the ability to act under pressure and assume responsibility under conditions of risk is a scarce commodity not easily developed in societies lacking a tradition of such management. It has proven to be easier to generate an oversupply of intellectuals, lawyers, and even doctors than to develop adequate cadres of managers and entrepreneurs.

These facts also tend to ensure middle-class status for such functionaries. Simple supply-and-demand analysis is hardly a full treatment of social reward systems; nor is rational planning a characteristic of all societies. But those societies that successfully expand the productive sphere, or seriously undertake such a venture, are generally characterized by an increase in the

[17] See National Manpower Council, *Government and Manpower* (New York: Columbia University Press, 1964), pp. 16–17.

[18] Kurt B. Mayer, "Social Stratification in Two Equalitarian Societies: Australia and the United States," *Social Research*, XXXI, Winter (1964), 451 ff.

[19] Chester Barnard, *Organization and Management* (Cambridge, Mass.: Harvard University Press, 1956).

[20] Homer G. Barnett, *Innovation* (New York: McGraw-Hill, 1953).

differentiation of overt rewards for such managers as compared to ordinary or skilled workers. Societies not making such adjustments or even decreasing the differential have failed to produce sufficient cadres. Most countries with *increasing* differentials are communist or socialist in nature. It is possible to argue that some of the increased financial rewards are compensation for lessened *ideological prestige in a "workers state"* and are meant to stimulate new sources of managerial talent. Advanced industrial societies seemingly have more leeway and can apparently adjust in the opposite direction—moving to equalization—without obvious effect so long as the general configuration is not seriously affected.

Rational calculation of life chances can never be so precise that small adjustments of rewards will generate precise, proportionately linear increases of numbers. Generally the lead time for training is the most significant aspect of such a calculation; the chances for success, the number and quality of rewarded positions, are shrouded by the mysteries of passing time. Adam Smith long ago argued that most men are over-optimistic about the future or are willing to gamble for improved status, a fact which makes lotteries and careers possible. The inducements necessary to make people undertake long periods of training involve compensation for advantages lost during the training period, but of course the one need precisely balances the other. In attempting to compensate societies may move to make the training period less of a sacrifice as readily as they move to improve the possible gains after training. No doubt this idea lies at the heart of extensive Soviet support for students—including family allowances.

Even more striking is the Castro proposal to abolish universities and supplant formal training with on-the-job training. Factories, he explained, would be workshops of learning as well as experience. Such a proposal would of course have the merit of eliminating one of the most fertile sources of social revolution or change, the university, and would also disperse a social group that has served as catalyst for many South American revolts, the students. But it also, if feasible, would minimize the differentiation between workers and managers, doers and theorizers, by approximating the social environment of a regular producing member of society for its trainees. Such an arrangement might also mean that less compensation would be necessary.

In general, however, it must be said that there are important functional arguments for believing that increased differentiation of educational facilities, rather than less, is likely and that differences of some kind will persist. Thus, the differences between bureaucracy and population, though not necessarily taking a specific shape or form, would, on the basis of this argument, represent in some guise a class difference involving some deferred recompense for additional skill and training.

Figures from the U.S. Civil Service Commission classify approximately 60 percent of their posts as white-collar. The long-range tendency of

government employment has been toward increasing numbers and proportions of white-collar workers in civil service as opposed to the government's
blue-collar "wage-board plans"; until recently at least there has also been a
tendency toward a higher-level classification. This in part represents the
natural human tendency to seek higher status so that the entire structure is
subject to what has been called the "grade creep." Slowly, over time,
positions are upgraded in much the same fashion as monetary inflation.
However, some of this routine upgrading represents new definitions of duties.
The move away from wage-board positions is a less contaminated measure of
increasing middle-class growth. Further, intensive studies of long-range
trends—Fabricant's on the United States[21] and Abramovitz and Eliasberg's
on England—are in clear accord on these trends.

Beyond the general proposition that bureaucracies' employees require
greater training than average, we can discern a tendency to require precise
specializations in large number. Fiscal control and organizational accounting
are obvious examples; the government needs accountants to control itself at
the same time that it requires them to control others and impinging
organizations. Lawyers are obviously and universally over-represented in a
governmental bureaucracy, but technical experts—engineers, physicists,
doctors—are needed in surprising numbers.

Certain functions are assigned to government as monopolies or near
monopolies. This may be because their nature suggests a need for social
control, or because the scale of operation requires vast investment, or indeed
for any reason deemed reasonable by the society. Percentages of warfare and
crowd control specialists found in government service are more than found in
the general populace because military and police are prime objects of public
service—virtual monopolies—in almost every known society. Such programs
as hydrogen bomb development and moon rocketry are sufficiently uneco-
nomic so that their specialized development is almost inherently governmental. Thus, virtually every physicist in the United States today is said to be
dependent on federal funds for some of his income; a surprising number are
direct employees.

Insofar as the bureaucracy requires large numbers of generalists and
legalists, it shares the attributes of legislatures and courts. These individuals
provide valuable services in communicating across governmental lines. It is
by no means rare for decision-level bureaucrats to seek and secure legislative
positions or judicial-appointments. Conversely, defeated office-seekers may be
consoled by an executive appointment. Such natural liaison is especially
valuable in a loosely-integrated government like the American system.

But the bureaucracy also supplements elective representatives insofar as

---

[21] S. Fabricant, *The Trend of Government Activity in the U.S. Since 1900* (New York: National
Bureau of Economic Research, 1952).

**TABLE 3.2    Distribution of Selected Occupations in Congress and the Higher Civil Service**

| Occupation | 89th Congress | Civil Service |
|---|---|---|
| Agriculture | 9.3% | 3.6% |
| Business-Industry | 27.5 | 2.9 |
| Education | 8.6 | 1.1 |
| Law | 57.0 | 7.0 |
| "Public Information" | 6.7 | 0.9 |
| Engineering | 1.3 | 17.5 |
| Physical sciences | 0.7 | 18.7 |

Source: Roger H. Davidson, "Congress and the Executive: The Race for Representation," in *Congress: The First Branch of Government*, ed. Alfred DeGrazia (New York: Anchor Books, 1967), p. 384.

members of the scientific community and other specialists and technologists seldom found in elective office are concerned. R. H. Davidson's evidence of this (Table 3.2) is relevant here. Such representatives of the "scientific estate" bring a point of view and an expertise not heard at the primary level of political decision-making. The total picture, therefore, remains one of relative underrepresentation of specialists of all types except lawyers. Without the bureaucratic corrective it might be an impossible situation.

## V. ATTRIBUTES

By attributes we mean qualities which are either present or absent (not as continuous variables) and in fashion subject to little or no control. Thus a person's sex is an attribute in our society, even though biologically it has continuous features and occasional surgical operations provide exceptions to the rule. Eye color is similarly treated as an attribute while hair color can be classified in either manner since it is changeable almost at will.

Skills are subject to manipulation and augmentation; they may be increased or decay. Governments may encourage or even force their increase or change. Attributes are less malleable, less the creation of their possessor, and, therefore, ultimately of his rulers. Maldistribution of skills throughout a population can therefore be expected to yield in time to rational public decisions. Change in attributes is much less to be expected for it requires drastic population measures—control over life and death—beyond the range of authority of most governments.

Many distortions of representativeness are produced by governmental needs. Age distribution is relatively fixed, for example. Obviously, infants and those in their training years are as underrepresented in the public service as they are in the labor force generally. Because women are generally less represented in the labor force and in many instances require extended leaves for childbirth, they could be expected to be and actually are less represented in public service.

Just as the peculiarities of governmental functions may differentiate those in the executive by skill and training, so they may also require other attributes. For example, a certain height is a prerequisite for police service in most societies. Sex and/or caste membership may be required for specific services in a way not required for private service. In history there are few women combat generals though Joan of Arc proved there was no physical basis for this convention. Even more striking is the historical paucity of women symphony conductors or composers. In some instances the social requirements of one society may spill over to another. For example, American diplomats have to be chosen with a view to satisfying the classification of acceptable attributes in other societies. The use of women or Jews in the Moslem countries of the Middle East appears as an absurdity or insult to them, while their avoidance exemplifies prejudice or archaism to at least majority sentiment here.

As it specifies the attributes necessary for governmental position, a society defines some of its values in a precise way. Employment criteria can be an index to social priorities much like government budgets are themselves valuable social indicators.

Insofar as a society specifies not attributes but continuous variables (and even combinations of variables), the society exhibits flexibility and sensitivity to individuals over gross classification. In a sense, this is contained in Sir Henry Maine's notion of the progress of society from status to contract as well as E. Adamson Hoebel's modification that progress has more the characteristics of evolution toward procedural justice than toward contract characteristics.[22]

## VI. INTERESTS AND PERSONALITY STRUCTURE

Abraham Lincoln is said to have endorsed a volume by writing "those

[22] Sir Henry Maine, *Ancient Law* (London: J. Murray, 1905), esp. p. 174; and E. Adamson Hoebel, *The Law of Primitive Man* (Cambridge, Mass.: Harvard University Press, 1954), pp. 327–29.

who like this kind of book will find it just the kind of book you like." Positions and careers are also matters of taste and attitudes. Recruitment for specific positions depends at least in part upon the potential job-holder; without proper attitudes on his part one cannot lead him daily to the office, much less make him think. Not everyone wants to work for governments just as governments do not open up all spots for every man.

Victor Thompson suggested "ideal type" officeholders, "bureaupaths" and "bureautics"—those who seek out and love the complexities of red tape, on the one hand, and those who oppose and hate such arrangements on the other.[23] Whatever the applicability of Thompson's formulations, it seems empirically true that American government employees differ at least slightly from the police in their evaluation of job security and predictability of career lines. While this may be a product of job experience, it seems likely it is also an independent cause for the reason for their service rather than its result.

If there are bureaucratic types (or perhaps even a single type), it is not likely that they are uniformly distributed throughout the population. In any event those personality traits which would constitute bureaucratic types would themselves set off the bureaucracy and would likely be densely concentrated there.

Cultural and class characteristics would also be involved. Much as Greek-Americans disproportionately turn to restaurants and confectionaries or Germans to beer brewing, there is reality in the stereotypes of the Irish policeman and politician, the Southern career army officer, and the Black postal clerk. Of course, ease of recruitment, friends, the grapevine of information, and familiarity with procedures should ease the way for access to high governmental service. Edward Banfield and James G. Wilson have found that certain groups have a greater propensity to vote for referenda for public purposes—a propensity they conceptualize as "public regardedness."[24] It is clear that certain families and groups have similar propensities and traditions of public service. We can think of the Adams family, which contributed major national officeholders from the eighteenth into the twentieth century, and the more recent example of the Kennedys.

The main outlines of this thesis are borne out in the American civil service. The middle-class professional-"salariat" origin of bureaucrats is confirmed by numerous studies. High-level officials of the United States are four times more likely to have professionals as fathers, and five times more likely to have a businessman as a father than chance would dictate.[25] Yet, perversely, they are not especially likely to have parents in the civil service.

[23] Victor Thompson, *Modern Organization* (New York: Knopf, 1961), p. 24.

[24] Edward Banfield and James G. Wilson, "Public Regardedness as a Value Premise in Voting," *American Political Science Review, 58,* December 1969, pp. 876–87.

[25] W. Lloyd Warner et al., *The American Federal Executive* (New Haven, Conn.: Yale University Press, 1963), p. 12.

Indeed, a comprehensive study finds they are drawn considerably less from such parents than are a similar sample of business leaders.[26]

This latter finding may be a major reason why the American civil service has not achieved the cohesiveness and continuity said to characterize the British and French bureaucracy. But even so, a predominance of certain cultural patterns and attitudes can be assumed from the disproportions noted. This predominance may be less than in some comparable structures, but it still is very important in its own right.

It is also important to note that personal success in bureaucracies is often a product of life styles. The correct manner, speech, and overt skills, coupled with an understanding of the nuances of the game plus a desire to win it (especially within the bounds of those nuances) comprise a recipe for success under normal conditions. It is, therefore, very likely that unrepresentative attributes will be characteristically even more pronounced in upper echelons of a service exhibiting such qualities at lower levels.

## VII.  THE INTRUSIONS OF LARGER PURPOSE

An organization is even less an "isle entire of itself" than an individual. Organization requires and involves commitment, interconnections, complexity, and interchanges. Such transactions do not end with the simplistic balance of accounts of the cost accountant or the naive utilitarian. The exchange of surplus commodities postulated by Chester Barnard and Herbert Simon (and his associates) as the basis of organizational structure is certainly not a one-shot transaction. The calculations of advantages offered involve not only utilitarian and psychic satisfactions but also future advantages. Similarly, an organization's transactions with others involve reciprocities, expected and implied promissory notes, and carry-over of obligations from one sphere to another.

In short, it is not merely the needs of the enterprise and those of potential employees—not even abuses of those—that determine organizational membership. Distortions from randomness occur because other demands, other purposes, other designs, and other priorities impinge on choice of personnel. Public bureaucracies are hardly immune; indeed, in many ways they are even more susceptible than others to such extrinsic claims.

The federal bureaucracy, for example, is itself a composite of organizations with corresponding sets of demands. These demands can affect employment conditions and advancement opportunities. Demands for efficiency, or merit, or skill can become secondary to the need to reward seniority in another (or even in the same) unit. An individual may be transferred from another position or appointed in the first instance.

[26] Warner, *The American Federal Executive*, p. 29.

Conditioned as we are to civil service pieties this may seem irrational or exceptional and certainly a departure from good practice. The thesis here is that such selection process practices are virtually inevitable, are quite rational, and can hardly be said to be "particularistic" in Weberian terms or any departure from the burgher-like virtues of universalistic criteria.

We can distinguish three ideal situations: (1) a hierarchy-command system in which the will of a small number of individuals can compel modification of employment practice; (2) an interorganization structure in which by political bargaining and overall interaction decisions by the unit at issue about its own hiring are examined and resolved; (3) an interaction of organizations at which surpluses are exchanged implicitly or explicitly. Under all three circumstances some modification of what is for the unit at hand an optimum employment pattern can be anticipated.

Where hierarchy is at stake, the interests of the decision-makers, as Mancur Olson has demonstrated, will coalesce with those of their following only in some respects—if at all.[27] The coincidence of interests of a specialized unit with that of the decision-makers is even less likely. Where there is power to change at will (or as near to it as we get in this world), the interests of the unit are likely to be sacrificed. In particular, the factor of loyalty becomes more relevant. Kings (like the Tudors) or dictators (like Hitler and Stalin) have valued personal loyalty over narrow efficiency and have proven that sufficient political power can depress the consequence of even total failure of a program. By minimizing the factor of loyalty, the democratic bureaucratic state makes possible closer approximation to representation of the total spectrum of the public. Requiring only loyalty to the regime—the enduring system of government—and arguing only for professionalized functional loyalty to existing officeholders and programs, the civil service state excludes only those clearly in rebellion against the system. (In recent years if one judged by rhetoric alone, one would suspect that in modern America even this minimum loyalty was not a condition of employment.) Personal loyalty is a highly restrictive, not to say ephemeral and emotion-laden criterion, so that its imposition is a severe tax on objective efficiency. Indeed, Montesquieu argued that kings were so affected by fears, misapprehensions, and a congenital susceptibility to flattery that public officeholding would be improved by offering positions for sale. (Voltaire scathingly noted that Montesquieu was perhaps influenced in this discussion by public criticism of a relative for such a purchase, and his personal reaping of some of the benefits.)

Where decisions are made from a larger-unit point of view, whether by simple political negotiation or "rationalistic" decision engineering ("Mac-

---

[27] Mancur Olson, *The Logic of Collective Action* (Cambridge, Mass.: Harvard University Press, 1965).

Namerization") or more realistically by some mix of these processes, some exterior modification of personnel policy should result. From a larger-unit point of view, the balance that should ultimately be struck is the expected marginal cost of a slight diminution of efficiency as opposed to the expected gain from the policy. Transferring rather than firing old-time employees in a division to be closed down may not seem desirable to a bureau chief who gets five slightly sub-par older men instead of the alert beginners he hoped for. To the divisional chief it may be very clear that this is a small price to pay for job satisfaction and maintenance of morale among his more than 23,000 employees. If a strike is avoided by this transfer, the logic may seem even more compelling.

Where two structures exchange benefits the same logical process can be expected, although the method of balancing the books is slightly different. It may well pay both sides to have Alpha National Bank directly or indirectly foot the bill with Beta Motors' hiring of C when it would slightly prefer to hire D, given efficiency needs. C may be a nephew of the president of the bank, a good but not spectacular lawyer. Particularly if the need for a loan is great, and the legal work routine, Beta may find its way to moving its retainer from its present first-rate lawyer. Again, we might have a situation of impossible tension between two vice-presidents at the bank, both with long-term contracts. It might well be profitable for the bank to pay all or part of the salary of one to function in a company in which, say, it has investments. We could multiply examples, but the fact remains that it may be profitable to effect changes in personnel policy of another unit. This results from at least three major considerations: (1) the difference in interests of the decision-makers of a unit and the "objective" efficiency welfare of the unit itself; (2) the marginal cost of inefficiency of the unit may be more than offset by the gain to some other unit; and (3) the cost of the personnel modification may be concealed or problematic, or delayed in its effects so that short-range gains may seem to predominate.

Whether we treat the American federal bureaucracy as a command, negotiating, or bargaining structure, it is clear that personnel policy is a compromise among the immediate unit needs, those of the total structure, and societal demands, as modified by decision-makers' needs and interpretations and overt manifestation of political power. Veteran's preference to public office is, as Walter Seal Carpenter pointed out, older than civil service. It represents in part the sheer political influence of a large and relatively organized class of citizens, and in part a sense that it is cheaper to employ a veteran in a position than to provide outright relief. A bonus on the qualifying exam may or may not mean a truly inferior occupant will take office. In any event, the public as decision-maker does not overtly experience the costs. Further, as John Miller argues, government is expected to carry "its fair share" of a social cost.[28] Quite similarly, public policy on minority-group representation is clearly reflected in federal employment. Nonwhite employment in the federal bureaucracy is in excess not only of nonwhite percentage of the general population, but even of the work force. (Nonwhite women disproportionately find it necessary or desirable to seek employment.) Similarly, women and the elderly find public service a more desirable work situation because of overt policies against discrimination—policies not always implemented fully but at least on the books. These policies are often resented by personnel officers who see them as threats to the integrity of their mission to hire "the best available" candidates. Such resentment is in fact one of the political and practical constraints on articulation of even more extreme public demands.

At a lower level, we may note that political connections seldom constitute a handicap for aspiring bureaucrats. Nepotism remains a common phenomenon in public service and a millionaire senator's son may turn up in a program intended primarily for underprivileged youth. Less objectionable perhaps are claims made in the name of geographic or political distribution. These almost invariably reflect political units, not population (every state gets one, and none more than five). Insofar as political power is malapportioned, officeholding will tend to reflect some similar malapportionment.

Where the tradition of civil service is stronger than in the United States, the impact of such criteria will be less. In the many nations where it is weaker, the consideration of unit efficiency may be of secondary importance, or virtually none at all.

## VIII. THE BUREAUCRACY ITSELF: THE SELFISHNESS OF STRUCTURE

The experience of government service itself constitutes a factor setting its membership aside from the general public. Where and how they work and other entrained consequences of such memberships further sharpen and differentiate the public service from the public they serve.

These differences are not inconsequential. On such matters as salary, job security, and maintenance of programs, the interests of bureaucracy are at least potentially sharply set apart from those of most members of society. A systematic study of the Illinois legislature found it very responsive to most political activity but impervious to all political pressure on one topic—reapportionment—where in a sense the legislator's own job security was at stake. These findings seem a fortiori, if not a priori, to apply to a more insulated body.

[28] John F. Miller, "Veterans' Preference in the Public Service," in *Problems of the American Public Service*, ed. Carl Friedrich (New York: McGraw-Hill, 1935), pp. 243–336, esp. pp. 279–87.

The bureaucracy's relationship to legislative and other decision-making groups also sets it apart. Its closeness to the seat of power makes it both more responsive and more response-producing than the average. Usually this will result in an augmentation of direct influence far beyond the one-man, one-vote principle. It need not, however, redound to the benefit of the public servant. Closeness to the seat of power may well provoke restraints rather than opportunities; the historic creation and use of eunuchs is perhaps a sufficient case in point. Closer at hand is the example of the American system in its attempts to curtail the political activity of civil servants precisely because of fears they might prove too potent, or become too politically committed one way or the other. The price then of one form of influence may be the giving up of another.

Those factors of personality discussed previously as differentiating recruitment may also be a result of the bureaucratic experience. It has been hypothesized that the structure of organization and the resultant experience results in peculiarly bureaucratic personalities, shaped in small but accreting ways over time. Less esoterically, we can suggest the cumulative experience will have some consequences setting off the group from others. As Michels, among other writers, emphasized, the attitude of those in preeminent structures creates differences in attitudes toward the public and of the mass toward the official as well. Prestige and deference—or noticeable lack thereof—inheres in the office in ways different from other roles or positions.

Bureaucrats, in short, as bureaucrats, are *per se* different. No one, it appears, is sufficiently fond of officeholders to say "vive la difference." Those advocating some form of participatory democracy or radical representativeness in public leadership must, therefore, by definition attack the problem by rotation in office, sharing of the function, or some other form of debureaucratization. To date it has not been possible to reap the objective advantages of rationalized professional structures through unstructured, amateur efforts. The history of revolutions against bureaucracies is that they merely substitute new structures, largely manned by the same people, for those that were the causus belli.

## IX.  CONDITIONS OF RECRUITMENT

The bureaucracy is not parthenogenetic. Recruitment is an ongoing process that involves reciprocal attractiveness and mutuality of interests before cooptation and acceptance of roles takes place. But patterns of recruitment, like all patterns, take on shapes and therefore inevitably have consequences for different strata and different people.

Recruitment is inevitably a function of high-level administrators. We have already suggested the domination in such structures of those with high-level skill. We can generalize further. The higher the level, the more dominant middle-class and advanced skills. The people who design civil services have within themselves some of the quintessence of civil servants. Their bias is toward formal educational requirements, written exams, and the piling up of various proscribed attainments easily measured, cumulatively scaled, and easily evaluated. This operates to the advantage and convenience of the recruiting administrator, for ease of administration is clearly desirable. Disqualifying and even artificial requirements are useful in limiting the number of applications that must be processed and seriously considered. Exceptions, waivers, temporary appointments, and special titles can if necessary be arranged.[29]

But formal requirements beyond necessity, which are almost inevitable concomitants of administration, are also unconscious defenses of value systems, a vindication of the achievements and values of the top echelon. The organization shapes the man as he rises and he uses his achieved power to perpetuate the mold. H. R. G. Greaves claims evidence that those who were promoted from the ranks in Britain were not superior in initiative and skills but in conformity.[30]

The tendency to formal requirements may reach the level of almost impassable barriers as in Confucian mandarinism in a society overblessed by candidates, or it may take the milder forms of unnecessary educational or irrelevant written performances as in the American system.

Such arrangements are not only advantageous for higher officials. Generally, incumbents are reluctant to welcome competition or to recruit superiors. The introduction of higher standards for newcomers with "grand-father clauses" exempting incumbents is the usual history for bureaucratic entry.

Modes of entry are not the only obstacle to employment. There must be vacancies. These are subject to the vagaries of life and are hardly continuous or automatic. Agencies have vacancies when they are created, absorb new functions, or have new resources allocated to them. Beyond this, removals or withdrawals are necessary. Withdrawals are subject to the whims of the officeholder—and acts of God (even more whimsical it appears, for "few die and none resign"). Removals are more difficult in practice than in theory. By and large even revolutionary purges have concentrated on key changes rather than inefficient widespread removals.

Lack of control over positions is accentuated by these factors and lack of control over resources. The financing of administration depends upon others; like vacancies it can be sporadic or episodic.

---

[29] E.g., see Ivar Berg, "Rich Man's Qualifications for Poor Man's Jobs," *Trans-action*, VI, March (1969), esp. p. 46 reporting a study of the National Industrial Conference Board showing that job requirement qualifications vary by the academic calender, i.e., by supply.

[30] H. R. G. Greaves, *The Civil Service in the Changing State* (London: G. G. Harrap, 1947), pp. 65–66.

Who is or becomes available thus depends very much on timing beyond the control of the organization. Thus surges and losses must be adjusted to. This often means greater resources become available in times of prosperity, when competition for able personnel is at its highest. The cyclical nature of vacancies itself unnaturally limits the range of personnel recruited, particularly in smaller agencies. The higher ranks of the American civil service, for example, face unusual depletion in the next few years as the generation of New-Deal–recruited administrators retires. Such a wave of withdrawal of a particularly able group—Washington was then the center of all action— makes the task in a more competitive era doubly difficult.[31]

Once within an agency, there is a certain tendency to identify and continue within it. To the degree that an individual's fate is bound up with that structure, there is a concomitant sense of protection of its positions and of sharing in its fate.

Information about openings and patterns of information about recruitment follow restricted patterns as well. Visits to colleges and other recognized massings of large groups of available manpower have restrictive implications. Individuals in a position to evaluate and validate training will have special influence in recruitment and placement. Until 1919, candidates for the foreign office or diplomatic service had to be "personally known to the secretary of state" or recommended to him by "men of standing and position on whose judgment he could rely." [32] The human tendency to aid friends and relatives, as well as the social reality that training and habituation in styles of behavior tend to be class-conditioned and passed on from generation to generation, threaten constantly to restrict access to such positions. The term nepotism—that is "nephew-ism," probably a euphemism for "natural" sons—arose over governmental favors extended among ruling families by members of the family in a position to do so. This human tendency exists in the restaurant business and in the professions, and in twentieth-century America is most conspicuous in—of all places—the building trades, such as the plumbers' union. But this restrictiveness, or more probably family indulgence, is of more social concern on the public level. We may laugh at the explanation of young Hilton's success—"my father ran into me in the lobby of one of his hotels and took a liking to me," but find such explanations inadequate and even dangerous as a basis for public office.

Restriction—or its opposite, expansion—of access to office can often be most effectively accomplished through changes in access to higher education. "Old boy" recommendations for admission to schools are less obvious, more private, but more effective than a denial of a right to compete. Soviet changes

---

[31] See "Men Who Really Run Washington," *Business Week*, Aug. 3, 1968, pp. 62–68.

[32] Quoted in Donald Kingsley, *Representative Bureaucracy* (Yellow Springs, Ohio: The Antioch Press, 1944), p. 127.

in scholarships and preference in education opportunity were correctly interpreted by sociologist Alex Inkeles as heralding the highly rigid Russian society of the 1960s.[33] The Northcote-Trevelyan Commission on the other hand recognized that to change the social composition of the bureaucracy a change in the role of "the state as educator" was equally necessary. The British example has been the conscious and sometimes unconscious model for other societies' parallel efforts which have usually involved much more than class differences, as in the American dream of the assimilating power of the public school.[34] The contemporary American drive for equality for Blacks and Chicanos explicitly recognized the need for simultaneous and concerted efforts at enforcing voting rights, changing employment pattern, and gaining access to effective education of the minorities.

Such a vital and almost universal linkage between social advance and educational level is in a sense a "confession in avoidance," one which leads to a paradox. Only through education can greater equality for all groups be achieved through maximum liberation of individual talent. But this, of course, is achieved through enhancing some over the achievements of others.

## X.  SUMMARY AND CONCLUSIONS

Organizations with tasks require certain skills and types of persons to carry out those assigned purposes. In the end this provides a limit on the representativeness of bureaucracies. The limit is a fragile one, perhaps less well defined than many writers have suggested. Bureaucracies can make adjustments in functions, rearrange some duties to create positions, permit sinecures, appoint not-quite-qualified persons, and bide time while creating skills. But the limit surely exists—above all the limit that bureaucrats per se are different. And so far at least human society has invariably found them preponderantly middle-class.

[33] Alex Inkeles, "Social Stratification and Mobility in the Soviet Union: 1940–50," *American Sociological Review*, 1950, pp. 465–79.
[34] See Rupert Wilkinson, *Gentlemanly Power* (London: Oxford University Press, 1964).

# 4

# *How Bureaucracies Can (and Should) Be Representative*

## I. INTRODUCTION

We must conclude from Chapter 3 that bureaucracies are inherently unrepresentative and cannot be microcosmic reproductions of total society. Once that truth is established, we must reevaluate our reasons for pursuing this topic. Why consider the impossible dream in scholarly work, especially in an era in which every semieducated actor or short-story writer or tin pan alley rhymester is willing, even eager, to lay down eternal truths and his solutions for all societies?

The first and shorter answer is to note that the bureaucracy is still at least potentially more representative than other arms of government and that in at least some senses it does in fact manage to be just that—more representative than other units. The second and more complex answer is that for a variety of reasons it is important for bureaucracies to approximate representatives even if they never fully achieve it.

The first answer has, to be sure, some of the aura of "tu quoque" or

63

"you're another." The bureaucracy can be called representative simply because it is more broadly based than other clearly nonrepresentative structures. Nevertheless, this inclusiveness—if generally true—constitutes a sociological fact of importance.

The second answer rests in part on the first. It stresses the functional desirability of just that state of affairs. The virtues of bureaucratic representativeness are similar to the claims made for legislative representativeness with respect to its *consideration* of policy. We would include several advantages that are superficially the same as for legislatures: the comprehensive presentation of formulations of view (political representation) and of types of evidence (functional representativeness). It also involves bringing multiple perspectives into the process of consideration and decision. The many minds brought to bear may not guarantee the best decision but they clearly guard against the worst—the ignorant or the blind leap into action.

With respect to acceptance of decisions, bureaucracies have certain inherent advantages. Diffusion of a policy, explanations of the reasons, and general exhortation are usually best advanced by a broad-based group with access to many strata. Again, a profusion of skills adds to the simple political and geographic advantages the technical possibilities for mustering support. Further, legitimacy can be said to inhere in such a multifaceted structure. Indeed, if a society wishes to claim objectivity and impartiality, no better argument can be advanced than that its officers embody in their personalities—and very being—proof of just that objectivity and impartiality. This legitimacy may or may not be associated with particular policies; it clearly transcends any single question. It seems certain that long-term confidence in the pattern of decisions enunciated by a structure is closely related to its reputation for permeability. Traditionally, the Black community's suspicion of the police is a standard example. Parallels to this particular expectation can be found in the sharply different expectations of objectivity in different cultures found by G. A. Almond and S. Verba (see Table 4.1); these expectations closely parallel patterns of bureaucratic openness or restrictiveness.

The point must not be overstressed, however. A sense of restricted participation need not be accompanied by doubts about performance. Fire departments in the United States have been traditionally even more lily-white than police forces. Yet resentment of them—except for exclusionary practice—is far less, and as far as the written record would indicate, not at all common in the past. We can distinguish the two in several respects: fire departments have fewer practical effects on the daily lives of Blacks. They are generally associated with positive programs that almost always bring benefits rather than incursion of punitive aspects of policy. Furthermore, since the threats of fire can seldom be localized, fire protection is virtually a public good whose benefit has to be conferred rather equitably to all. Blacks suspect

**TABLE 4.1**  Expectation of Treatment by Governmental Bureaucracy and Police, by Nation (in %)*

| % Who Say | U.S. Bureauc. | U.S. Pol. | U.K. Bureauc. | U.K. Pol. | Germany Bureauc. | Germany Pol. | Italy Bureauc. | Italy Pol. | Mexico Bureauc. | Mexico Pol. |
|---|---|---|---|---|---|---|---|---|---|---|
| They expect equal treatment | 83 | 85 | 83 | 89 | 65 | 72 | 53 | 56 | 42 | 32 |
| They don't expect equal treatment | 9 | 8 | 7 | 6 | 9 | 5 | 13 | 10 | 50 | 57 |
| Depends | 4 | 5 | 6 | 4 | 19 | 15 | 17 | 115 | 5 | 5 |
| Other | — | — | — | — | — | — | 6 | 6 | — | — |
| Don't know | 4 | 2 | 2 | 0 | 7 | 8 | 11 | 13 | 3 | 5 |
| Total % | 100 | 100 | 98 | 99 | 100 | 100 | 100 | 100 | 100 | 99 |
| Total number | 970 | 970 | 963 | 963 | 955 | 955 | 995 | 995 | 1,007 | 1,007 |

* Actual texts of the questions: "Suppose there were some question that you had to take to a government office—for example, a tax question or housing regulation. Do you think you would be given equal treatment—I mean, would you be treated as well as anyone else?" "If you had some trouble with the police—a traffic violation maybe, or being accused of a minor offense—do you think you would be given equal treatment? That is, would you be treated as well as anyone else?"

Source: G. A. Almond and S. Verba, *The Civic Culture* (Princeton, N.J.: Princeton University Press, 1963), p. 108.

a really prejudiced engine unit might dawdle a bit, and there are stories of firemen letting houses burn to the ground as racial punishment. But both the fireman and the community would be aware that little of this is really possible. The danger of letting any fire go unheeded is self-evident. In the performance of their jobs fire departments are likely to be equitable in action regardless of the racial makeup of their personnel. In turn, perceptions of their conduct are likely to reflect both external realization of this logical expectation and the cumulative experience derived from the structured behavior likely to follow from such realities.

In short, representativeness is positively associated socially and objectively with more widely accepted solutions. But it can guarantee neither technically desirable decisions nor popular ones. It merely helps. But deleterious consequences can—and do—result from failure to recognize its claims.

## II. SIZE AND DIVERSITY

By their very nature bureaucracies can contain multitudes; at the very least they contain greater complexities than executive and legislative branches. Executives, even when loosely defined, range only slightly: from standard monocratic structures to the U.S. presidency's many hundreds of loosely articulated "staff" arrangements. Legislatures range a bit more in size but are still within pronounced limits. A city commission will number as few as five while national assemblies may run in the low thousands. At least when conceptualized in ideal terms, executives are supposed to be structured for quick decisions. Legislatures are compromises in size between the perceived need for representativeness and their capacity to reach closure on legislation. These idealizations limit size and diversification. The bureaucracy, however, is historically the result of executive mitosis. As an executive structure multiplies in purposes it grows in structural complexity and moves toward the border between direct and indirect executive control. In brief, a bureaucrat is an executive official whose office is now in a building not occupied by the chief executive. Historically, bureaucracy evolved much in that way: the king's small household units, directly responsible to and in daily contact with him, gradually acquired premises and semiautonomy over time.

These units, tributes to proliferated purposes of government, tend to acquire separate perspectives, often reflecting the segment of the public they deal with—their "clienteles." Beyond that, since these organizations have their own purposes, they require a variety of talents. We can list an incredible array of titles: from embalmers to cryptologists, cold-type composing machine operators, game law enforcers, prosthetic representatives, nuclear engineers, cadastral surveyors, cargo schedulers, and calibration and measurement quality-control inspectors—all of them specialties listed in civil-service descriptions. The advantages of numbers, plus the need for and possibility of specialization, result in the actuality of diversification. Those who seek publicly contested public office share some considerable measure of skill in dealing with the electorate. By and large they are generalists who can function as brokers. Specialists are few in the political branches, but in abundance in the bureaucracy. But the latter structure also must contain a stratum of generalists to coordinate policy and translate and mediate between policy makers and policy executors.

The difference both in types and in degree of homogeneity of types has important policy consequences. Reviewing British colonial policy, for example, a historian has noted some consequences of relying on the brilliant amateur, the classical scholar, for administration, and avoiding specialists like economists. Unable to interpret modern economic data, high-level administrators ignored or rejected proposals they could not understand from subordinates, particularly Nigerians, at home. At the same time, policies emanating from the colonial office—for example, to pressure companies to pay a groundnut price based on freight differentials—were shelved in fact because the appropriate officials lacked the technical ability to implement them.[1] Amateurs, too, often believe general principles will solve matters where a well-saturated expert knows unraveling of intricate detail is necessary. The Supreme Court of the United States, for example, has for years adjudicated cases under the interstate commerce clauses by deciding whether particular state taxes impede the flow of interstate goods. While in one sense the justices are clearly experts—many are elite lawyers—they share the profession's generalist cast and must deal with anything if it comes up in the proper legal form. Economists are fairly agreed upon the fact that the Justices' efforts to protect free flow of goods have been blundering, and ascribe this to their lack of economic sophistication. The Justices operate under yet another handicap—their need to tie policies to rational, nominally enduring principles—and cannot easily experiment and tinker with the adjustment of policies. Nevertheless, the lack of economic expertise is generally seen as a primary contributor to their lack of success, though some economists suggest that better-informed Justices have backed no more desirable programs than their less sophisticated brethren.

The failings of the expert are equally well publicized. His training, experience, and commitment reinforce habits of thought. Commitment to an area of expertise appears to be a major component of a sense of identity in a

[1] Eme O. Awa, *Federal Government in Nigeria* (Berkeley: University of California Press, 1964), pp. 171–72. See also Margery Forham, ed., *Mining, Commerce, and Finance in Nigeria* (London: Faber & Faber, 1948), pp. 122–24.

modern society comparable to religious, ethnic, and racial thinking. Fields of expertise and professions establish paradigms of thought. So long as accommodations to new situations can be effected within lines suggested by their approach, experts can be expected to be more precise, knowledgeable, and sensitive—in short, to exhibit expertise. But abrupt or radically new situations may confound the expert more than one who has not invested intellectual capital in a line of approach. The expert can be transformed into the nit-picking, overbearing, it-can't-be-done spokesman against pragmatic or new approaches.

A prime example of such expert stultification is to be found at universities. Control by the faculty (that is, by specialists) results in a high degree of precision and expertise. But reification of departmental and disciplinary lines is so intense that accommodation of new emphases, even when externally validated as valuable, is difficult in the university structure. Areas such as genetics, which crosses the discipline lines of biology and chemistry, have almost invariably been forced to secede to establish their own viability. Experiments in cross-disciplinary cooperation have been labeled as failures through application of standards of performance not necessarily invoked as against "old-line" departments.

The traditional hostility of old-line regular law courts to administrative agencies, especially in the United States, is another case in point. Though the flow of quasi cases to the agencies outstripped any reasonable capacity of the courts to handle them, the jealousy of the judges was immense because of the rise of what was in many ways a rival method of adjudication. The constitutional fight of 1937 was in part an effort to secure breathing space for agencies whose functional contribution was indispensable to orderly government in a complex society.

It is disturbing that these examples of myopia involve two groups with exceptionally strong value systems which are designed to maximize objectivity and minimize self-interest. Judges and professors often view themselves as just a little lower than angels. But they fight tooth and nail for their own when threatened. The value systems of other specialists place varying degrees of emphasis on internalized self-restraint. Professions like law and medicine will have more, while engineering or metallurgy a bit less. But the members' investment in time and effort almost invariably results in strong ego-identification with attributes of the system and with a severe loss of pragmatic objectivity.

Bureaucracies approximate specialist agencies more than any other branch of government. Indeed, an effort is made to specify each office with considerable particularity and to define specialties within each service that are comparable to such specialization in others. "The policy of civil service was based upon the assumption that government work can be classified into occupational groupings within vertical services." [2] These services are generally led by specialists sifted from the ranks in terms of their multiple capacities: (1) their technical competence—needed to judge and develop solutions and personnel; (2) their organizational skills in directing their own unit for task purposes and in maintenance of morale; (3) their capacity to relate and represent their own unit's purposes and needs both horizontally to peers in other parallel structures and vertically to superiors in their own, or, outside unit lines entirely, to other governmental branches or the public generally. In short, they are led by specialists who adapt generalist functions and styles.

On the other hand, legislatures and judiciaries are represented at juncture points by policy generalists, who pick up the skills of specialism for this leadership role. A chairman of a House committee gradually works his way into technical expertise, for example.

It is, therefore, not unreasonable to believe—though it is highly speculative—that habituation in amateur and generalist views can impair success in dealing with complex social problems, while specialist frames of mind sharply hinder new approaches. This is a generally accepted but hardly well-researched notion. Fresh and balanced solutions most probably emerge from tensions between types of thought, in the interplay that most closely resembles that in society. And if this analysis is correct, the governmental bureaucracy inherently is particularly likely to be innovative. Large size and diversity mean that such creative tensions more easily occur within its boundaries. In other structures such a dialectic normally involves action across agencies—a more difficult process. Frequently it means interaction with the bureaucracy anyway.

On the other hand, the fact of the bureaucracy's diversity and great size implies severe disadvantages to creative consultation. Bureaucracies are notoriously places where left hands do not know what right hands are doing. Because consultation of all is impossible in a large hierarchy, it becomes necessary to formally define who is to be consulted and who has the right to speak. All too often this is formulated on specialist lines. But specialties are predicated upon past experience so that there is a channelization into expected and established relationships.

The mere presence of diverse sources of advice does not mean they will be heard. On the contrary, amateur structures more decidedly differentiate responsibility and have gradations of power. Most clearly in legislatures and in the highest executive councils, most matters are still of general concern. Bureaucracy, however, is established precisely upon hierarchical communica-

[2] Fritz Morstein Marx, *Elements of Public Administration* (Englewood Cliffs, N.J.: Prentice-Hall, 1959), p. 36.

tion lines, and by definition, on the restriction of the authority to be consulted and to decide. Sententiously put, a bureaucracy depends upon the definition of who writes the memo, who gets the original, and who has access to the carbon.

## III.  SOCIAL STRAINS AND DIVERSITY

All social systems possess strains and conflicts. We may put aside here the dispute between those who see such strains as pathological and those who view them as signs of growth and creativity. These views belong with other antinomies of mankind and are probably matters of temperament and style rather than truly empirical queries. It is enough to note that nirvana is an unstable—if not nonexistent—state for a social system.

Sources of strain can be accommodated within bureaucracies more easily than elsewhere. Large numbers of employees allow accommodation of a larger range of interests than elsewhere. A greater variety of possible balances exists. There can be not only some numerical balance, but also some mix of status and power in complex fashion. Furthermore, functional specialization of units may be matched to group strains and demands in complex accommodations that are more acceptable because they are linked to such specialization. That the Secretary of Labor should be someone acceptable to the AFL-CIO is politically and psychologically tolerable; but if the unions controlled 10 percent of all senators, that would become an incendiary issue.

It has long been recognized that some accommodation proximate to the ruler was desirable where there are group strains. The harem was designed not only for the ruler's pleasure but also to provide a sense of access and involvement for divergent groups in the decision process. The history of marriages between contending royal families suggests both the symbolic and practical utility of such accommodations. The taking of hostages into the king's household was a less polite form of some of the same notions. The need to give employment to potentially dangerous rebels was repeatedly mentioned by witnesses at the Trevelyan-Northcote hearings[3] in a fashion similar to modern discussions of summer jobs for teenage Blacks. Keeping a trouble-maker where you can keep an eye on him and have a hold on him is a basic means of operation.

While modern bureaucracies do not completely span skill-based class differences, they can lend themselves easily to the glossing over or accommodation of certain other types of differentials. Generally, these are of the ethnic, religious, or cultural variety—particularly where these lines do not coextend to skill or aspiration differences.

---

[3] H. R. G. Greaves, *The Civil Service in the Changing State* (London: G. G. Harrap, 1947), p. 26.

The overt universalism of bureaucratic structures makes creed, color, birth, and ascribed (as opposed to achieved) status at least officially irrelevant. "Can he do it?" rather than "Who is he?" or "Who does he know?" is the order of the day. As we shall see, the latter questions can be bootlegged back into the discussion under the guise of the first—but the primacy of ability is itself of immense significance.

Bureaucracies by and large are probably less prone to accept artificial barriers than run-of-the-mill small enterprises in part because of their fundamental value system, in part because of their great need for talent. This is, however, not to gainsay the fact that complex structures can often disguise or insulate such practices if they are out to discriminate. The contempory notion of "institutional racism" captures some of this reality, pointing up the fact that such discrimination can be veiled from its very perpetrators if the consequences are not clear and if the officeholders are no more sensitive than most humans.

In general, bureaucracies have no difficulty in mobilizing the services of persons of differing sex, skin color, religion, or ethnic backgrounds. This is true even when fairly considerable hostility, aversion to personal or social contact, or even suspicion of motives attach to the differential background. Their structure emphasizes the impersonality of the process, the cloaking of the officeholder in the authority of other: "I salute the uniform and not the man." Similarly, they are functionally specific: "If I catch him in civies, I'll even up the score." The force of authority and the precision and limitation of its overt scope permit accommodation of behavior with a minimum of cognitive dissonance: "I do what I have to in the office; he's in charge. But I know him for what he really is. They can't make me like him." Indeed, the emphasis upon the precise, official requirement simultaneously exerts immense psychological pressure to conform while permitting the escape valve of personal evalutation outside the job. In short, bureaucracies operate to emphasize prescriptive, universalistic authority and minimize nepotic or clanlike ties—precisely as described by Weber.

For some structures there is even special moral pressure to become representative. Those agencies whose enunciated purpose is to confer benefits generally and whose function requires considerable personal interaction in the community at large will generally be under greater pressure—both internal and external—to be more inclusive. Functionally, the argument that they will be more effective will have great weight. Morally, the suggestion that greater objectivity and fairer distribution will ensue will have some impact. And from a public relations and political point of view, it will be evident that the agencies' clientele group and support base must be the beneficiary groups. The more broadly they can define those groups—for example, to include middle-class agency employees who share some overt characteristic with large numbers of beneficiaries—the more the agency benefits. Inasmuch as the respectability of client groups is a source of political strength, the agency can gain at both ends of the political spectrum.

This, too, should not be exaggerated. Bureaucracies are timid structures not inclined to wage against-the-odds struggles. City Hall is perhaps even less disposed than anyone to fight City Hall. As Nazi Germany and Soviet Russia best demonstrated, existing bureaucracies can be utilized to effect radical regime change. While bureaucrats cannot be replaced as a class, individual members are easily dispensed with. Gradual turnover of personnel, accompanied sometimes by ruthless requirements that the disposed officer train his successor, can, over a reasonably short period of time, with relentless purpose—slackening only for necessity or policy considerations—succeed in virtual 100 percent turnover. Only in elite structures, particularly the military and especially the intelligence agency and in foreign offices, was there appreciable failure to score rather rapid clean sweeps.[4] Certainly, personnel officers will adhere pretty much to standards prescribed for them. Overt discrimination or other standards of selection are matters of relative indifference to them. Above all, the professional value system of personnel officers emphasizes their own instrumental role in implementing the standards of selection set by those in authority.

Furthermore, the channels of organizational life provide a highly effective invisible screen behind which artificial selectivity can take place without much awareness of it on anyone's part. The very labyrinthine structure is a source of filtering and choice. The forms of application, the way in which announcements are made, and the informal channels which constitute a major, if not *the* major, source of recruitment can operate to enhance or diminish participation.

## IV. RELATIONS WITH THE ENVIRONMENT: THE EXAMPLE OF MULTILINGUALISM

Where a multilinguistic environment exists, the burden is real and external, one that must be borne by the society in some manner. Either bureaucrats individually or through a division of labor become multilingual, or the populace does, or some service is in effect curtailed or rationed. The multilingual requirement becomes a burden in a society in which most transactions could be satisfactorily carried on in either language or a combination of them, but in which for mixtures of convenience and symbolism either or both sides become obdurate about their linguistic rights

---

[4] See Fredric Burin, "Bureaucracy and National Socialism," in *Reader in Bureaucracy*, ed. Robert Merton (Glencoe: Free Press, 1952). For a different view, see E. N. Peterson, "The Bureaucracy and the Nazi Party," *Review of Politics*, XXVIII, April (1966), 186–87 and esp. p. 189: "The party never had the trained personnel to take over state offices."

(or rites). A badly divided society will have as a symptom a linguistically burdened bureaucracy. But language may also serve as a barrier in government when it is not in fact a social issue of great importance.

When such considerations are involved difficulties arise whether one wishes to acknowledge realities or not. Social cleavage has bureaucratic consequences. The typical attitude is that only dysfunction follows form. A Canadian observer reflects this attitude:

> Modern bureaucracies ideally require social eunuchs who have been neutralized as persons within their own societies and who have divested themselves of interests in social groups and institutions involved in the struggle for power. Since the bases of power associations are frequently ethnic, regional, or religious, the idea that these groups should be "represented" in the bureaucracy contradicts the notion of the official as the servant of the state. Ethnic, regional, and religious affiliations are not rational qualifications for office. Therefore, in the fully developed bureaucracy, and in its elite, one would expect to find these groups represented in about the same proportion as they are to be found in the general population if the following assumptions are met: that educational facilities to meet the qualifications are equal as between regions, religions, and ethnic groups; that no rights to offices are denied on ethnic, regional, or religious grounds; and that there is equal motivation in these groups to become public servants. Where higher offices are disproportionately distributed we do not know, without further investigation, which of these assumptions have not been met.[5]

In a footnote Porter suggests even more emphatically that these questions are fundamentally irrelevant to Weber and presumably to all scholars:

> It can be argued that national unity is a rational aim within the context of the wider social system, but if so, it is like salvation, one of those other-worldly goals which Weber would consider as *wertrational*.[6]

On the whole Porter frowns upon such "irrationality"—what he quotes Alexander Brady as calling "a tactful balance of national elements." As he points out, when such appointments are made in full consciousness by the authorities, the minority bureaucrat will to some extent be forced to regard himself as representative of his group. But as Donald Rowat noted in an exchange with Porter, this is a product of a total picture; the attitudes of the majority decision-makers create or reflect a situation which produces such behavior by the minority.[7]

[5] John Porter, "Higher Public Servants and the Bureaucratic Elite in Canada," *The Canadian Journal of Economics and Political Science*, XXIV, November (1958), 490.

[6] Porter, "Higher Public Servants," p. 490.

[7] Donald C. Rowat, "On John Porter's 'Bureaucratic Elite in Canada'," *The Canadian Journal of Economic and Political Science*, XXV, May (1959), 205.

We have already noted the conflict between various levels of service about definition of purpose and have indicated that this has costs. We are now weighing the advantages of considering such factors—and they are, in my view, overwhelming. Porter's view is that national unity is, like salvation, a factor to be ignored in governmental structure, one to be subordinated to such momentous considerations as the ability to score two extra points out of 500 or the ability to operate an additional office machine. The protective ideology of civil service insists upon purity at all costs. But it is difficult to see this as anything but a form of the bureaucratic myopia said to be characteristic of such structure. "What profiteth a man if he gains a mote, and loses the whole world?" The preoccupation with neutrality was a protective device to minimize extra-unit considerations in an era of temptations. But it surely is a middle-class fetishism to say "let the civil service rules be followed though governments—though the heavens—fall." Here a reexamination of ends and means, a close balancing of claims, is more rewarding than supercilious recital of slogans; from the standpoint of effectiveness of governmental units at all levels, the receptivity of the public to its employees may well be a factor in hiring. The description of immediate unit needs as "universalistic" and desirable, while other considerations are called "particularistic" and irrational, ignores the question of perspective. Indeed, what we have is a series of criteria which can be viewed as belonging in either category depending upon the perspective adopted. We may for societal reasons or for other considerations choose to ignore certain factors or to include others without being in the least irrational. In fact, societies everywhere do and should exclude "for reasons of public policy" all kinds of considerations—age, marital status, etc.—with respect to employment.

It is clear that in other ways bureaucracies are concerned with popular effectiveness. Indeed, they devote rather considerable resources to this purpose. Over a period of years, starting with the forest service in 1909, Congress has forbidden the use of agents to extol their departments without specific legislative authorization. Legislation in 1913 and 1923 confirmed this nominally blanket denial.[8] But in fact thousands of civil servants are involved in various forms of public relations work. Further, their documented activities have included efforts to stimulate public demand for universal military training and to increase demands for appropriations of many kinds, as well as public educational campaigns that have reached millions.

The government also pioneered in and directly contributed to the growth of public opinion research as a tool for understanding and influencing mass opinion. Press releases are hardly the only form of effective public relations. Helping John Wayne make a movie or Efrem Zimbalist, Jr., a TV

---

[8] See J. A. R. Pimlott, *Public Relations and American Democracy* (Princeton, N.J.: Princeton University Press, 1951), pp. 69–139.

series, sending out speakers to articulate State Department points of view, and having Federal Reserve Board employees read learned papers at meetings all supplement more obvious forms of creating public receptivity. Eugene Litwak and Henry J. Meyer, in an arresting discussion of more complex ways of securing compliance and agreement, have suggested even more indirect methods: they point to such arrangements as the "detached expert," the street gang worker, the county agent, the Soviet agitator (an institutionalized office), or the neighborhood "worker priest" as examples of such efforts.[9] Cooptation of local opinion leaders, either as "detached experts" or in some more indirect way, is a standard device. "Settlement houses" or other community service arrangements which service clients while spreading the message are common arrangements. Relations with voluntary associations are other common devices: the armed forces and veterans' associations, the State Department and foreign policy associations, and the like. The relationship may even be more overt. The Department of Agriculture helped establish the Farm Bureau; connections between the County Agent and the Bureau remained official until recent decades, so the editors of *Fortune* could with justice write as recently as 1944 of the Bureau as "a private lobby sponsored and supported by the government it seeks to influence." [10]

Similarly social workers strongly suggest—to a point approaching coercion—that clients join established client organizations which are indeed useful in maintaining welfare-recipient self-esteem and efficiency but which also serve the unit's political purposes. Meyer and Litwak supplement this with notions of "common messenger," "formal authority," and "delegation" to subsidiary groups such as auxiliary organizations.

These all exist to a striking degree. The point is that the image of the bureaucracy as neutrally enforcing a policy without regard to the environment is inadequate. Even Philip Selznick's sophisticated and influential discussion of organizational "cooptation" implies (or, more fairly, has been generally used to imply) a passive state. Selznick emphasized the degree to which TVA was forced to modify its national goals by local pressures and was thus "coopted." [11] It was this interactive, reactive aspect that captured attention. Similarly, Herbert Kaufman's *The Forest Ranger*[12] emphasizes the organizational devices and socializing process for its agents by which the forest service seeks to immunize the rangers from such pressures.

But Litwak and Meyer draw attention to the degree to which bureaucratic services do actively attempt to change the political environ-

[9] See Eugene Litwak and Henry J. Meyer, "A Balance Theory of Coordination Between Bureaucratic Organizations and Community Primary Groups," *Administrative Science Quarterly*, XI, June (1966), 31–58.
[10] "The Farm Bureau," *Fortune*, XXIX, June (1944), 157.
[11] Philip Selznick, *TVA and the Grass Roots* (Berkeley: University of California Press, 1949).
[12] Herbert Kaufman, *The Forest Ranger* (Baltimore: Johns Hopkins Press, 1960).

ment. The perspective they give to some apparently neutral operations indicates a great deal of such activity goes on in somewhat disguised form, since it has been regarded as bad form for organizations to create their own demands. Indeed, channeling and controlling such efforts must be a significant aspect of maintaining responsive and responsible government.

If diffusion of policy information and active intervention by agencies are in fact a major ongoing aspect of bureaucratic operations, then it seems to follow that the bureaucracy's structure should allow for effective carrying out of this function, and its choice of personnel should—among other competing and sometimes overriding considerations—consider employee attributes or memberships where relevant. Organizations should do so in aggregate terms in considering and evaluating their overall policies of recruitment and maintenance. They seemingly should do so in the concrete case, by dealing with specific individuals, where clear and definite needs and advantages are involved. There may be overriding advantages to ignoring such factors, but this should be determined as an end-product of rational evaluation, not by shibboleths of pseudorationalistic thinking.

## V.   DEMOGRAPHIC AND NONPOLITICIZED REPRESENTATIVENESS

We have already argued that the realities of societal division of labor and the facts of nature limit representativeness of administrative units (Chapter 3). But paradoxically and dialectically, the reverse also seems self-evident. The inclusiveness of the bureaucracy gives it advantages in representing inchoate groups and elements of society not normally involved in policy-making. Elective structures are emphatically the crystallization of articulate, organized, and recognized operative political groups of various types. The topsy-like giant conglomerate that is a national administration probably includes a broader spectrum of the divorced and the benedicts, the ugly and the beautiful, male and female, young and old—of groupings we quickly think of but do not normally see as political units, as well as others we do not think of at all in connection with public issues. We may make an imperfect analogy: the advantages of the bureaucracy over the elective arms of government are similar to the advantages of a random sample of the population over a stratified sample. It is freer, less limited by existing political lines, and more responsive to emergent or evanescent political cleavages.

Age differentiation, for example, is usually better represented in administrative structures. Career lines can begin earlier than in elective office, which tends to be a reward for party performance, requiring multiple years of service and therefore age. Senators must, by law, be thirty, for example (and are therefore presumptively not to be trusted). In fact they are generally much older, from limited social groupings, and by various measures far above the population mean.

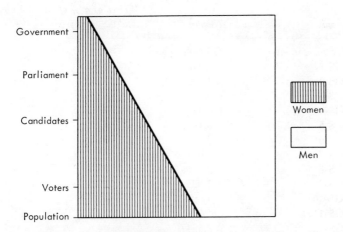

**FIGURE 4.1      Political roles of men and women**

Source: Maurice Duverger, *The Political Role of Women* (Paris: UNESCO, 1955), p. 123.

Sex differences are pronounced in political advancement. The relative absence of women in office is greater the higher the position. While this pattern operates for both political and administrative posts, it seems even more pronounced in the former. In 1955 Maurice Duverger suggested the pattern of female participation in government and politics shown in Figure 4.1. This pattern is remarkably borne out in the distribution of women in the American federal service in 1959 (see Table 4.2). There is some indication that women find it particularly difficult to secure the support of women for political office.[13] It is also, of course, no easy task to overcome male stereotypes. Nevertheless, impressive changes have occurred. In 1967, for example, the comparable figures for women's employment still showed the same general structure, but revealed pronounced increases in Grades 15 to 18, with almost a sevenfold increase in the number of women in these grades in less than a decade; the proportion of women in such positions virtually doubled as well.

As Duverger has also noted, however, these higher-level posts are not uniformly distributed, being concentrated in conventionally approved roles for women, for example, social service. Over 20 percent of these posts (184 of 859) were in Health, Education and Welfare, which has only 5 percent of all

[13] Maurice Duverger, *The Political Role of Women* (UNESCO: Paris, 1955), p. 89.

**TABLE 4.2    Women in the Higher and Lower Ranks of Federal Government in 1959**

| Ranks | Number | Women as a % of total GS employees |
|---|---|---|
| Total women | 476,448 | 49.1 |
| GS-1 | 946 | 27.7 |
| GS-2 | 23,652 | 52.4 |
| GS-3 | 119,276 | 68.7 |
| GS-4 | 114,921 | 70.7 |
| GS-5 | 68,199 | 62.2 |
| GS-6 | 25,248 | 54.0 |
| GS-7 | 30,021 | 33.1 |
| GS-8 | 5,496 | 22.1 |
| GS-9 | 13,825 | 13.8 |
| GS-10 | 1,494 | 10.6 |
| GS-11 | 5,974 | 7.5 |
| GS-12 | 2,634 | 4.5 |
| GS-13 | 1,158 | 3.1 |
| GS-14 | 351 | 2.2 |
| GS-15 | 90 | 1.2 |
| GS-16 | 9 | 1.0 |
| GS-17 | 7 | 1.8 |
| GS-18 | 2 | 1.3 |
| GS-18+ | Not reported | |
| Grade not specified | 63,145 | |

Source: Employment Statistics Section, USCSC, Washington, D.C. Figures are for October 31, 1959. Included are all women in white-collar positions, employed full-time under the General Schedule salary system, both in the United States and abroad. Figures for total employment taken from Table A-6, p. 26, *1960 Annual Report*, USCSC.

employment and about 7.5 percent of all female employment. When classified by occupational group, 145 or nearly 17 percent are in social science, psychology, and welfare, which involve less than 2 percent of all employees and an even smaller proportion of all females.

### Policy Diversity and Policy Continuity

Bureaucratic structures operate in symbiotic relationships with interest groups. They are enforcers of policy—often involving regulation of specific groups—yet are dependent upon those regulated for support. It is likely that the more discretion accorded the agency, the more overt and complex the mutual dependency. There is also some evidence that American political culture accentuates this relationship, but it is also clear that it is not unique to American agencies.[14]

Administrative units also become ego-involved with policy enforcement. They develop a sense of commitment. Indeed, such a sense of purpose is a sign of health in an administrative structure and its absence is a sign of morale decay. Not only is the vigor and the future of an agency inextricably linked with particular policy patterns, but its very sense of identity is sometimes also at stake.[15]

The bureaucracy is therefore identified with many groups and is the repository of policies of divergent eras and divergent majorities. It therefore potentially can be more representative than the current majority or plurality dominating legislative or political executive life. In the interstices of bureaucratic agencies and subagencies, those identifying with policies and programs of the past may often be found. Opponents of Hitler were fairly entrenched in Admiral Canaris's Abwehr until the bitter end. More conventionally, the objectives of the Third and Fourth Republics are pursued by still-operating French functionaries. The antitrust division of the Department of Justice still reflects old populist views of size and concentration even in Republican administrations, while the Federal Trade Commission operates more in the Hoover-Mellon tradition of benign fostering of capitalistic growth even under liberal Democratic presidents. The interests of farm shippers may be pursued by the Department of Agriculture while the railroads are encouraged and abetted by an agency all-too-frequently theirs and not the public's watchdog—the ICC.

It is easy to see in this persistence of old policies and bureaucratic rivalry only archaism and inefficiency. But clearly it has its utility. Issues too complex or narrow to engage the normal political channels may be so represented. Furthermore, cyclical majorities are supplemented and kept from too-sweeping a control when narrow margins are temporary or nonintense. Of course this has implied costs, against which these advantages must be set. Continuity is one thing; rigidity, though related, is also disastrously different.

[14] See Joseph G. LaPalombara, *Interest Groups in Italian Politics* (Princeton, N.J.: Princeton University Press, 1964) and Samuel Beer, *Modern British Politics: A Study of Parties and Pressure Groups* (London: Faber and Faber, 1965).

[15] See Marver Bernstein, *Regulating Business by Independent Commission* (Princeton, N.J.: Princeton University Press, 1955).

TABLE 4.3    **Full-Time White Collar Employment by General Schedule and Equivalent Grades Worldwide**

| Grade* | Employment Total | 31 October 1967 Women Number | % |
|---|---|---|---|
| 01 | 10,817 | 7,740 | 71.6 |
| 02 | 50,660 | 40,025 | 79.0 |
| 03 | 153,287 | 118,601 | 77.4 |
| 04 | 227,820 | 142,319 | 62.5 |
| 05 | 574,184 | 170,123 | 29.6 |
| 06 | 113,003 | 51,462 | 45.5 |
| 07 | 145,781 | 49,969 | 34.3 |
| 08 | 41,852 | 9,058 | 21.6 |
| 09 | 162,304 | 36,130 | 22.3 |
| 10 | 23,209 | 2,833 | 12.2 |
| 11 | 144,063 | 15,316 | 10.6 |
| 12 | 118,180 | 7,448 | 6.3 |
| 13 | 85,308 | 3,623 | 4.2 |
| 14 | 42,938 | 1,583 | 3.7 |
| 15 | 22,901 | 577 | 2.5 |
| 16 | 6,321 | 124 | 2.0 |
| 17 | 2,349 | 35 | 1.5 |
| 18 | 756 | 5 | .7 |
| Above 18 | 609 | 15 | 2.5 |
| Ungraded | 6,168 | 2,417 | 39.2 |
| Total* | 1,932,510 | 659,403 | 34.1 |

*The grades or levels of the various pay systems have been considered equivalent to specific general schedule grades solely on the basis of comparison of salary rates, specifically, in most instances, by comparing the 4th step GS rates with comparable rates in other pay systems.*
** *Excludes employees of Central Intelligence Agency, National Security Agency, Board of Governors of Federal Reserve System, and Foreign Nationals Overseas.*

Source: "Study of Employment of Women in the Federal Government, 1967," Bureau of Management Services, U.S. Civil Service Commission, Statistics Section, 1968.

## VI.  CONCLUSION

We may summarize: variety begets variety. The very size and diversity of the bureaucracy encourage further diversity. This is not to deny that selectivity and artificial restraint have characterized administrative units. But such discriminatory selection has almost uniformly reflected similar, almost invariably harsher, political disabilities. Because of its size and visibility, government service can be a good index of the degree to which a society is open to talent rather than a vehicle of restricted group power.

And in its greater potential for representativeness the bureaucracy has an unusual opportunity and responsibility for societal integration and community-building. The emphasis of Weberian claims for political neutrality, and subsequent reiteration by the epigone, has been on sterility, gray anonymity, and functional specificity. The perfect bureaucrat, it has been reiterated, is like the traffic light which performs only its functions—no more and no less—without regard to personalities or influence. Any departure from this automatism, "the machine model" in March and Simon's terms, is treated as a departure from perfection. The less creative he is, the less he exhibits initiative, the more he is faceless, the fewer excess skills the bureaucrat brings, the greater he would be deserving in the eyes of these writers.

The essence of the argument of this chapter is the suggestion that the human potentialities brought by bureaucrats to their jobs are inevitable and advantageous. Far from being solely liabilities they may have advantages that far outweigh the alleged—and exaggerated—benefits of neutrality. What is really sought is not cold-fish indifference but responsiveness to political direction, an acknowledgement of democratic political supremacy. But surely the principles supposedly involved in Leninist democratic centralism would suffice, that is, freedom to advocate until a decision is reached but solid and enthusiastic acceptance and support thereafter. The qualities of judgment, information, and fervor that bureaucrats do bring as they aid decision-makers are in fact resources of immense social advantage, not merely weaknesses men are heir to. In particular, the bureaucrats' affinity for the population has great potential advantage for social stability and increased bureaucratic responsiveness. We may ask the paradoxical question, "Neutrality for whom?" And we may replace it with a more realistic and purposive program of a representative, effective, and responsible bureaucracy.

# 5

## Some Patterns of Bureaucratic Representativeness and Misrepresentativeness

We have suggested that societal conflicts will usually be mirrored in bureaucratic disputes. The necessity for day-to-day interactions in bureaucracies literally aggravates such conflicts. Those cleavages which create tensions in the broad societal arena make cooperation difficult in an organizational context. Above all, there must be trust before there can be effective joint enterprise. Societies with troubles will have troubled bureaucracies. It is to a concrete examination of that proposition that we now turn. And though it is uncontestably true that "for instance is not proof," neither are examples a denial. In short, we can generalize only from the multiplication of instances, and derive abstractions from the concrete.

We shall examine a series of problems and patterns of bureaucratic interaction in an effort to determine their effectiveness in minimizing social conflict and in maximizing bureaucratic effectiveness.

## I.  INDIA: CONSTITUTIONAL PROVISIONS ON REPRESENTATIVENESS

The complex problem of overcoming what is generally regarded as the most perduring of caste systems has challenged the ingenuity of India's leaders. On the whole, recent years suggest that they have managed to deal with the problem with fair success.

What is involved is the well-being and progress of a group numbering some 64.5 million in India's 1961 census (nearly 80 million in 1970), a group considered to be lower caste, persons whose touch is defiling. Because the Government of India Act of 1935 listed them in a separate list of schedules, they sometimes are referred to as "scheduled castes" and this term is sometimes distinguished from the term "backward classes" (formerly called "depressed classes") which is also used comprehensively to include Harijans as well as others.[1] In general, the Harijans (Gandhi's term suggested to replace untouchables; it means "children of God") are ill-defined. Caste standing is a complex matter of occupation (with lower castes, of course, in the most menial tasks) and other forms of social behavior including place of residence and dietary habits. The gradations are multifarious. In all, the "backward classes," in the broadest sense of this phrase, potentially include 30 percent of the population. Fully 2,399 communities were qualified to be involved in the administration of the program for such groups.[2]

In former years, rigid caste lines were reinforced by social acceptance and social habit. The untouchables were serfs hedged in by interminable restrictions against wearing silk, drawing water from a village well, entering a Brahmin temple, or living within village boundaries. The British freed them from some disabilities, and modern urban life makes others unenforceable. Yet their basic situation remains unenviable and a challenge to an Indian democracy, which must reconcile this estranged one-fifth of its population.[3]

The chief methods used are rather direct. Constitutional and legal provisions provide for machinery to aid the disadvantaged. The constitution contains a series of prohibitions and provisions, drawing upon nearly a century of British legislation intended to eradicate Harijan disabilities. It enjoins equality before the law (Article 14) and prohibits caste discrimination in government service, but permits reservations of places for scheduled and backward classes (Article 16); it reserves for ten years (later extended in 1959

---

[1] See, e.g., Lelah Dushkin, "Scheduled Caste Policy in India: History, Problems, Prospects," *Asian Survey*, VIII, September (1967), 626ff.

[2] See J. H. Hutton, *Caste in India*, 4th ed. (Bombay: Oxford University Press, 1963), pp. 192–222.

[3] See the excellent discussions by Jones, Béteille, Srinivas, Mayer, and Bottomore in Philip Mason, ed., *India and Ceylon* (London: Oxford University Press, 1967).

for another ten years) places in both parliament and state legislatures for scheduled castes (Articles 325, 330, 332, and 334), and prescribes no caste discrimination in admission to public educational institutions. The state is enjoined to protect and promote the interests of the "weaker sections of the people" and a special officer to promote safeguards for scheduled castes, a commission for backward classes, and a method for defining scheduled castes are all provided for (Articles 46, 338, 340, and 341).[4]

These arrangements were precedented. The early British practice had favored community representation and had inaugurated such elections in 1909. Gandhi opposed (by "fasting to the death") extension of such a system to Harijans because he felt it would contribute to even greater separatism. "Sikhs may remain as such in perpetuity, so may Muslims . . ." Gandhi argued, but "would 'untouchables' remain untouchables in perpetuity? I would far rather that Hinduism died than that untouchability lived." [5] This resulted in the Poona compromise of 1932, later incorporated into the Government of India Act of 1935. The untouchables were guaranteed a minimum number of seats within the Hindu constituency but were otherwise maintained in the broader electorate. The 1950 constitution continued the system, guaranteeing Harijans 76 positions and state legislative seats roughly proportional to their population. Other minorities were given protection in other and complex ways. The 1961 election law is retrograde as to community lines by clearly designating Harijan and non-Harijan seats, thus clearly separating the communities in the way Gandhi feared.

The system guaranteed that there would be one scheduled caste member from each district. In a few instances, caste members achieved both top positions and the courts held they were entitled to both seats.[6] It would appear this led to the electoral change. Yet, as Dushkin points out, the infrequency of double-election of scheduled caste members is the surprising fact that emerges over a decade. "An inspection of a number of the returns," she concluded, "indicates that the main reason this happened so rarely is that many non-Scheduled Caste voters simply did not cast their second (reserved seat) ballot." [7]

The original constitution contained no provision for special admission into educational institutions. After a supreme court ruling that no reservations of places for underprivileged groups was permissible, the constitution was amended. Besides differential admission requirements, favorable fee arrangements are also in common use. Governmental concessions even go

[4] Marc Galanter, "Law and Caste in Modern India," *Asian Survey*, III, November (1963), 544, provides an excellent summary of these provisions.

[5] Quoted in Dushkin, "Scheduled Caste Policy in India," p. 631.

[6] Enid Curtis Bok, "Constitutional and Judicial Provisions for Progressive Discrimination in India" (unpublished).

[7] Dushkin, "Scheduled Caste Policy in India," p. 634 and 634n.

beyond this. Roughly half of the governmental expenditures for scheduled castes is for education, one-quarter for housing, and the rest scattered. Since 1955 a number of severe penalties attach to offenses against untouchables and the onus of proof is on the accused if the accuser is a member of the scheduled castes.[8]

The use of quotas for government service is not rigid, but sets aside positions for those who might qualify. This also was based upon British practice in their effort to keep the Brahmins from monopolizing positions allocated to natives. The 1909 efforts by anti-Brahmin Indians first crystallized latent Indian feeling and cohesion. The result was a complex recognition of community and strata privilege under the British and this established the pattern for postindependence India.

In the years after 1950, the backward class quotas were by and large ineffective. This was particularly true regarding qualification for the upper reaches of the bureaucracy. While at lower rungs the Harijans exceeded their quota, they fell far behind in positions requiring educational achievement. Beginning in 1962 or 1963, however, the education policy began to be felt as significant numbers of Harijans began to fill their allotted higher-level class posts.[9] While this was accompanied by a complex of differently calculated scores, it is by no means clear that this reflects real deterioration in an overformalized and largely irrelevant testing process.

This development has not occurred, however, without costs. On the interpersonal level, it has aroused the inevitable personal hostility predictable when individuals with identical performance records are treated differently. But resentment of high-caste Indians has not been sufficiently dysfunctional to be drastically disruptive, and indeed the low-caste Indian is still about as likely to be dissatisfied with the government's efforts (see Table 5.1).

From the standpoint of the underprivileged beneficiary, there are also costs involved. He gains his benefits by confessing and registering a low status, one which he may be seeking to deny and avoid. "Passing" in the American sense may take place by personal action or even caste-wide sociological reaction. Religious conversion is a form of discarding aspects of caste, while by a process dubbed by Srivinas "sanskritization," a caste may take on habits with a higher degree of prestige. (The latter was a traditionally approved method. "Sanskritization seems to have occurred throughout Indian history and still continues to occur." [10] Geographic mobility was often a form of social mobility; the same caste may have a different social standing or a pretension to it in different parts of the country.)[11]

[8] Dushkin, "Scheduled Caste Policy in India," pp. 626–27.
[9] See A. Béteille in Mason, ed., *India and Ceylon*, p. 105.
[10] M. N. Srinivas, *Social Change in Modern India* (Berkeley: University of California Press, 1967), p. 1.
[11] Srinivas, *Social Change in Modern India*, p. 97.

**TABLE 5.1    Social, Education, and Income Group Differences in Public Evaluation of the Job of Central Government Officials**

|  | Doing a Poor or Fair Job | | Doing a Good or Very Good Job | | Don't Know | |
|---|---|---|---|---|---|---|
|  | Rural | Urban | Rural | Urban | Rural | Urban |
| *Caste Groups* |  |  |  |  |  |  |
| High Caste | 21% | 49% | 59% | 37% | 21% | 15% |
| Middle | 24 | — | 48 | — | 27 | — |
| Low | 15 | 38 | 62 | 45 | 21 | 16 |
| *Education Groups* |  |  |  |  |  |  |
| Illiterate | 22 | 30 | 47 | 43 | 29 | 27 |
| Primary | 15 | 47 | 62 | 28 | 23 | 25 |
| Middle | 19 | 48 | 70 | 34 | 11 | 18 |
| Highest | 23 | 56 | 73 | 41 | 4 | 3 |
| *Income Groups** |  |  |  |  |  |  |
| Under 50 Rupees | 20 | 16 | 50 | 62 | 29 | 23 |
| 51–100 | 21 | 40 | 55 | 35 | 22 | 24 |
| 101–200 | 15 | 43 | 63 | 39 | 22 | 18 |
| 201–300 | 19 | 47 | 57 | 43 | 24 | 10 |
| Over 300 | 30 | 60 | 61 | 33 | 9 | 7 |

* Based on monthly family income.

Adapted from Samuel J. Eldersveld et al., *The Citizen and the Administrator in a Developing Democracy* (Scott, Foresman and Company, 1968), pp. 36–37.

Privilege for the underprivileged operates against this mobility. By forcing the low-caste Indian to state his lack of privilege to gain a privilege, Indian society is not only being paradoxical, but also apparently arouses some resentment among lower-caste Indians who feel they are being in some sense blackmailed:

> To obtain the privileges designed to elevate and transform the untouchable, he must affirm that he is one. The price of discrimination in reverse has been a kind of blackmail in reverse; in return for access to opportunity and power, the untouchable is asked to incriminate himself socially. This is not only profoundly disturbing but also an important source of alienation and rebellion.[12]

[12] Lloyd I. Rudolph and Susanne Hoeber Rudolph, *The Modernity of Tradition* (Chicago: The University of Chicago Press, 1967), p. 150.

The more systemic results are difficult to assess, enmeshed as they are in the total picture of transfer of control from the British to self-rule. The concomitant unimpressive showing of Indian self-government may be cause or effect or independent of this effort to eradicate the age-old inequities of the caste system. It is evident that the Indian public service has not been especially effective. Even such a close and friendly observer as Chester Bowles has pessimistically predicted the breakdown of the system and imminent anarchy. The educational system has become moribund, with routine memorization of irrelevant relics of British culture emphasized, while students press continuously for ever-lower standards.

There is, however, little inclination on the part of Western observers to blame these failures on the equalization program. The inability of the elitist civil service in the early years to effectively penetrate through change or policy continuity into Indian society was as dramatic a failure as later events. There is no indication that the press to convert Indian education into a cram course for bureaucratic office was led or even differentially abetted by lower-caste students. These tragedies might just as well have occurred for other reasons. There is little disposition by observers to blame India's woes on one of its few forthright and progressive programs, particularly when problems such as simple incompetence and indifference are rife and clearly involved. Indeed, even the Indians themselves were optimistic that the new stage reached in 1963 would herald more positive results, not just in the distribution of positions, but with respect to both quality of decisions and social responsiveness to governmental action.

It is generally agreed that the greatest weakness of Indian government has been its lack of penetration, that is, its inability to translate action within the political system into response at the societal level. The efforts to achieve a greater degree of representativeness in the bureaucracy would seem, then, to be a necessary if insufficient step toward achieving some capacity to secure receptivity and even multiplier effects for their decisions.

The British-created civil service was admirably suited to the "indirect rule" concept. The British maintained local law through local authorities, except that control was asserted by the British—again through coopted indigenous authority—when it suited the English overlords. David Low asked in 1964:

How is it that 760 British members of the ruling Indian civil service could as late as 1939, in the face of the massive force of Indian Nationalist movement led by Gandhi, hold down 378 million Indians? [13]

[13] D. A. Low, "Lion Rampart," *Journal of Commonwealth Political Studies*, II, November (1964), 235.

In large part the secret was the restricted control and impact actually implied in such a system. Without gainsaying the remarkable achievements of British India in the fields of medical care and technology, it seems fair to assess the purpose and execution of its rule and sovereignty as essentially highly limited. The British deliberately tried to maintain things as they were; they altered only what was necessary for British rule, or what was to their clear advantage, or what was necessary to avoid offense to their sensibility.

The modern world of development asks from government more positive and far-reaching changes. Alterations in the structure and composition of the Indian civil service seem called for, even should there be immediate costs. The policies already adopted in terms of welfare and social change probably exceed the system's bureaucratic capacities.

While they developed technical facility, the Indian subordinates were primarily, and purposely, oriented occidentally. That is, they were trained to carry out the relatively unambitious aims of a foreign power. By and large, the role appealed to the Brahmins and the British requirements (particularly the timing and manner of taking of exams and age of applicants) favored Brahmin candidates. They failed to develop the ability to deal with their real ambiance precisely because real power was elsewhere. They did not develop the means, will, style, and attitude necessary to implement large-scale social reform. Thus India, like most free and colonial countries, illustrates nicely the need for bureaucratic responsiveness and the argument for greater inclusiveness.

## II.  MALAYA:   UNIFICATION AND DIVISION

If the general costs—positive and negative—of representative bureaucracy are still unclear, its peculiar problems and costs in the former federated Malay States are most evident. It is not too much to say that the failure to provide more adequate sharing of control, wealth, status, and power led to the demise of the union. To this day, any indication of increased political power by the minority Chinese, even in a Malaysia separated from Chinese-dominated Singapore, arouses animosity and occasional riots.

The problem of the Chinese in Malaysia is the problem of the Chinese throughout Asia outside of China. Their efficiency, strong family structure, and qualities of drive and skill that make them disproportionately successful in the Orient arouse the suspicion, not to say hatred, of their neighbors. The Chinese are dispersed throughout Asia and the story is repeated over and over again. That they tend to be proudly separatist helps permit their treatment as sojourners rather than as permanent residents.

While there was contact between China and Malaya as early as the sixth century, and settlement of some 300 Chinese in Malacca in the early seventeenth century, the bulk of Chinese migration took place in the nineteenth and early twentieth centuries. Coming with the opening of opportunity in tin and rubber, they became the dominant non-European economic force in the area. Nonetheless, they remained a negligible political influence because they lacked a desire to "go native." "A Malay is an individual who speaks the Malay language, is a Muslim and displays a culture which, for all its variations, is clearly recognizable." [14] The Malays remained rural, cultivators and fishermen. The Chinese and Indians are densely concentrated along the west coast. For all their rural origins, the upwardly mobile Chinese have become urban, commercial, or, by a more complex route, mine workers and then owners.

After World War II, pressure began to build up—including bloody guerrilla warfare—both for independence and for an increasing political awareness by the Chinese. Concentration of those Chinese formerly rural furthered political consciousness. Independence was secured in a series of steps beginning with an abortive agreement in 1946 and a more successful attempt in 1948, culminating in elections in 1955 and independence in 1957. By agreement, the process of "Malayanization"—the substitution of natives for British high civil servants—was even more gradual.

Under the British no Chinese were admitted to the elite Malayan Civil Service until 1952 and in general, although Chinese representation was not small, it was highly concentrated in such services as medicine and other nonpolitical functions. Writing in 1937 Rupert Emerson reported in his classic book *Malaysia* that the British favored Indians and Chinese for routine positions disproportionately, but restricted key posts to Malays.[15] Continuation of this policy can be seen from data collected by Robert Tilman and presented in Table 5.2. These ratios are hardly biased in favor of the plurality of Malays in the population, shown in the 1957 census as 49.8 percent Malaysian, 37.2 percent Chinese, and 11.1 percent Indian. But, for example, nearly half (151 of 366) of the Chinese in administrative positions just prior to independence in 1957 were in the noncritical medical services; only 248 of the 684 serving in 1959 were in that service.

The Malays were sufficiently concerned to insist upon a provision directing the head of government to function "in such a manner as may be necessary to safeguard the special position of the Malays and to ensure the reservation for Malays of such proportion as he may deem reasonable of positions in the public service" (Sec. 153). Special scholarships were permitted on a similar basis, and Malay was made the official government language. In accordance with these provisions quotas of Malays to all

---

[14] Maurice Freedman, "The Growth of a Plural Society in Malaya," *Pacific Survey*, XXXIV, June (1960), 159.

[15] Rupert Emerson, *Malaysia* (New York: Macmillan, 1937), pp. 182 and 515.

TABLE 5.2    Total Division I Officers

|  | 1957 | 1958 | 1959 | Approximate % of population (1957) |
|---|---|---|---|---|
| Expatriate | 1,766 | 1,268 | 1,074 | — |
| Malay | 390 | 512 | 653 | 49.8 |
| Chinese | 366 | 520 | 684 | 37.2 |
| Indian | 213 | 298 | 396 | 11.1 |
| Others | 127 | 166 | 120 | — |
| Total | 2,862 | 2,764 | 2,927 | 100.0 |

Source: Adapted from Robert O. Tilman, "Public Service Commissions in The Federation of Malaya," *The Journal of Asian Studies*, XX, February (1961), 164.

non-Malays were established for the elite Malayan Civil Service at 4 to 1, while the External Affairs Service was limited to 3 to 1. Of the two junior administrative services, the Malay Administrative Service was limited to Malays. The Executive Service was open to competition. However, promotion was quite easy from the Malay Administrative Service and not even provided for from the Executive Service. The effects of these conscious efforts can be seen in Tilman's data on the Malayan Civil Service (see Table 5.3).

TABLE 5.3    Composition of Malayan Civil Service

| 1959 | 1960 |
|---|---|
| 104 Expatriates | 62 Expatriates |
| 166 Malays | 193 Malays |
| 28 Non-Malay Asians | 33 Non-Malay Asians |

Source: Robert O. Tilman, "Public Service Commissions in the Federation of Malaya," p. 194.

On September 16, 1963, Singapore, Sabah, and Sarawak were added to the Malayan Federation to form the Malaysian Federation. This exacerbated the problem, for which their heavy concentration of Chinese population, the plurality was now Chinese by about 42 percent to 40 percent Malay. While the old federation remained in Malay control, and the terms of union gave them the upper hand, the situation was precarious. In a tense society facing

Sukarno's constant threat of war, still further trouble was added by the community riots in Singapore in September, 1964. Even as they simmered down, they seemed to exacerbate latent fears and appear to have led to the split between Malaysia and Singapore on August 9, 1965.

"What collaboration has occurred has been for the most part among that thin upper stratum of Western-educated Chinese, Indians, and Malays, many of whom are civil servants," as James Scott has written.[16] In fact, as Margaret Roff points out, this has meant that almost all candidates for office and leaders have had to be English-speaking.[17] The irony of this situation is compounded by the constitutional position afforded the languages. The 1957 constitution affirmed Malay as "the national language" with English as a concurrent language for ten years, unless extended by Parliament. The Alliance led by Tunku Abdul Rahman has sought to keep peace by emphasizing Malay as indeed the "national and official language and English as a second language, while the languages of others will go on as they have been going on." [18] While maintaining adamantly that Chinese will not be an official language, the government's practice—but not policy—is to permit "explanations" in Chinese on official documents. The effect of the National Language Act of March, 1967, was to relieve some of the pressure on this issue by giving sufficient symbolic victories to the Malays with some reassurance to the other communities. However, many Chinese believe that it served the purpose of identifying the Alliance not in terms of its claims to be a multicommunal agent but simply as a mere subtle and conciliatory instrument of Malay dominance.

Similarly, the educational system has been effectively nationalized without affront to the language arrangements in these systems. The effect is that communal control and separatism are diminished without being attacked. But Chinese charges of discrimination in crucial gateway tests for students reflect deep doubts. Furthermore, as Karl W. Deutsch suggests, such doubts that anything will make them acceptable members of the community are fundamentally destructive of the polity:

> Familiarity may be sufficiently effective to permit the attitude of confidence and trust. (The opposite of such successful predictions of behavior are the characteristic fears of the alleged treacherousness, secretiveness or unpredictability of foreigners. Such fear of unpredictable "treachery" seems to be more destructive, as far as the experiences from our cases go, then to any clearcut and realistic expectations of future disagreements. . . .)[19]

[16] James Scott, *Political Ideology in Malaya* (New Haven, Conn.: Yale University Press, 1968), pp. 13–14.

[17] Margaret Roff, "The Politics of Language in Malaya," *Asian Survey*, VII, May (1967), p. 317.

[18] Roff, "The Politics of Language in Malaya," p. 317.

[19] Karl W. Deutsch et al., *Political Community and the North Atlantic Area* (Princeton, N.J.: Princeton University Press, 1968 ed.), p. 57.

From the Chinese point of view, their success at overcoming hurdles is constantly used, in defiance of previous promises, as the basis for creating new disabilities. At the same time the continued success of the urbanized Chinese and Indian students at the University of Singapore keeps Malay enrollment at only 25 percent, which lead to clamor by the Malays for further restrictions and quotas. The Chinese in turn are debating the advisability of a Chinese university with all that would be entailed thereby.[20]

One great eruption of Chinese-Malay tension occurred in 1965. Early in that year Lee Kuan Yew, Singapore's Premier, began his campaign for a "Malaysian Malaysia," presumably a more truly interracial community. Essentially he attempted to forge a leftist, Chinese-oriented opposition to the Malayan Alliance and Rahman's United Malayan National Organization.[21] Lee's campaign secured little change, and he began to hint at secession and regrouping of the various states. Finally, by a somewhat mysterious process, secession was mutually agreed upon. With this change the slight Chinese plurality ended and Malay predominance was assured for several decades.

The issue was never fully resolved with the rather quick annulment of the 1963 arrangement. By 1969 the ruling party coalition of Tunku Rahman was in difficulties with both major communities. In May, 1969, election results showed deterioration of the government majority, especially among the Chinese. Several opposition parties scored at the expense of the Malaysian Chinese Association, allied with the Tunku's Alliance party. The Association's announcement that it would not participate in the government set off racial rioting which resulted in curfew and suspension of the constitution.[22] The failure to achieve a balance through quotas has thus continued through several different forms of the federation, and through the transfer of leadership from Abdul Rahman to Tun Abdul Razak. By February 19, 1971, the crisis of 1969 had died down sufficiently to permit restoration of the constitution.

## III.  LINGUISTIC CONFLICT:  BELGIUM AND CANADA

Language can be, as we have indicated, both a cause and a pretext for conflict. Since separate languages are almost universally the ultimate thread of a separate and unique culture and nationality, they are seldom unique factors creating a conflict. Rather, a conflict over language tends to emerge from a pattern of social intercourse with more obvious reasons for discontent.

[20] See Cynthia H. Enloe, "Issues and Integration in Malaysia," *Pacific Affairs*, XLI, Fall (1968), 372.

[21] Justus van der Kroef, "Chinese Minority Aspirations and Problems in Sarawak," *Pacific Affairs*, XXXIX, Spring–Summer (1966), 78–79.

[22] See *New York Times*, May 12, 1969, p. 5, and May 14, 1969, pp. 1 and 6.

Given the pattern of existing social conflict, however, language differences may well be sufficient to serve not merely as pretexts for conflict but also as occasions. The flare-up of conflict may be the product of some symbolic act: an individual may be merely irritated by a policeman telling him to "move on" in the hated language of those dominant, ruthless "others" and thus precipitate an incident almost for its own sake. Or the groups may come to violent disagreement over the issue of the language of instruction and examination at official universities where quite real differences in concrete results may emerge or at least be reasonably feared.

Two countries with such issues are Belgium and Canada. In the former, the majority Flemish (about 55 percent of the population) feel put upon by the more aggressive, entrepreneurial Walloons who have tended also to dominate the political life of the country. The Walloons (about 35 percent of the population) speak French as do most of the people of Brussels who constitute about 11 percent of the population. The language dispute has sporadically further divided a country unsure of its boundaries, its self-respect (as in Nazi collaboration and lack of an underground), or its King. In 1962–63, a compromise was reached dividing the country into two linguistic zones. With this beginning Belgium has been gradually developing into a federated system under the guise of maintaining unity.[23] The balanced ticket of cabinet-making has been even more separate with Ministers of Education for the two regions.

Two remaining anomalies became the subject of political acrimony in 1968–69 in a crisis somewhat comparable to that of 1962–63. The University of Louvain with its French-speaking emphasis is north of the border line and the Flemings have argued that the 10,500 French-speaking students and faculty (as opposed to some 3,000 Flemings) threaten the Flemish character of the city. Similarly, they are unhappy at the migration of Bruxelois into traditionally Flemish suburbs with its possible implications for the school system. As for Brussels, the Flemish wish a 50:50 ratio in the public services on the grounds that it is the capital. The French-speaking Brussels' majority wishes to maintain the present 70:30 ratio.

After several cabinet crises, the issue has been temporarily resolved by linguistic concessions to the Flemings, economic concessions to the Walloons, and the promise of still further evolution toward federation and highly stratified and balanced governmental arrangements.[24] Louvain will transfer its French-speaking units, slowly over time, south of the border. Brussels suburbs will be Flemish no matter who lives there. On the other hand, economic measures to aid industries in Wallonia were adopted to offset the

[23] See Frank E. Huggett, "More Troubles in Belgium," *The World Today*, XXV, March (1969), 93–96.
[24] "Balancing Cash Against Language," *The Economist*, June 22, 1968, p. 25.

linguistic concessions. Not only was the cabinet divided 14 to 14 on a language basis, but separate ministries were added for relations between the communities and also for commercial development. Parity for the Dutch-speaking Flemings in governmental and military posts was also promised as a new goal.

In Canada, the issue is seen by some as an issue of "separatism" of the type encouraged, probably foolishly, by General de Gaulle.[25] Quebec's government has long been a focal point for such agitation. The effort to avoid French-Canadian nationalism has centered upon a call for "bilingualism and biculturalism." In these two countries there are indeed dual cultures and language is a discreet and distinctive index of separatism. The issue of whether French should be a *lingua Franca* is, as in Belgium, a vital one, albeit the shoe is on the other foot from one case to the other.

The linguistic demands are those of a community which represents about six million out of a twenty million population. More than eight million were of English stock. Numerous other groups, including the indigenous Indians and Eskimos, made up the rest—now about 27 percent of the population. Nationwide, with respect to language, 80 percent spoke English and 31 percent French, since about 12 percent spoke both. In Quebec 87 percent spoke French and only 37 percent English, whereas in New Brunswick 38 percent spoke French.[26] The localization of the issue, however, in some way exacerbates division, for geographic, religious, cultural, and ethnic causes coalesce in incendiary fashion.

By and large, however, the French Canadian is not actually French in outlook. Contact with France has been minimal and cultural contact even for French-Canadian intellectuals has been minor. The French-Canadian community was antiwar and isolationist in both World Wars, with little interest in the fate of either country.[27] Some evidence on this point can be adduced from an interesting experiment by the psychologist Leon Kamin. He polled Canadians on their preferences for nonexistent offices. Given a set of fake names respondents voted largely for party, when the pseudo-candidates were given a party label. In the group where even this party information was not available, voters chose by ethnicity of the name. They were in agreement in distinguishing between English and French-Canadian names, but were quite as emphatic among French Canadians in distinguishing between Canadians and French French.[28]

[25] See, e.g., "Bad Manners, Bad Politics," in *The Economist*, July 29, 1967, p. 397.

[26] "Equality of Opportunity and Pluralism in a Federal System: The Canadian Experiment," *International Labour Review*, XCV, May (1967), 396.

[27] W. E. Greening, "French Canada and France," *Contemporary Review*, CCXIV, January (1969), 20–23.

[28] Leon J. Kamin, "Ethnic and Party Affiliation of Candidates as Determinants of Voting," *Canadian Journal of Psychology*, XII (1958), 205–13.

To a large extent the French Canadians have been outside the dominant Canadian culture and currents of power. They have clearly been less than proportionately represented in mass communications, industry and finance, and education and public service. In part this is both a cause and effect of French-Canadian cultural differences and aspirations.

The program of the Liberal Party, since MacKenzie King and even earlier, has been to harmonize the two cultures. The pattern of party leaders who represent alternation of language backgrounds is symbolic of this attitude, as was the new flag decision made by Prime Minister Lester Pearson. In 1963 this effort took the form of the Royal Commission on Bilingualism and Bi-Culturalism, which was instructed to consider ways of building "equal partnership among the two founding races."

The grievances developed with respect to the public services were twofold: (1) the symbolic usage of the English language, and (2) total representation in the bureaucracy.

English has been the official language since the Treaty of Paris of 1763. The British North America Act of 1867, however, confirmed the right to use French in Quebec and endorsed its use as a second language in legislation and courts. The French Canadians seek to extend its use to a fully official language in all bureaucratic and other dealings; they argue that otherwise they are at a disadvantage. "I want my language to be respected in public places, particularly in federal offices" was a constant refrain in the report by the Royal Commission on Bilingualism and Bi-Culturalism.[29]

As part of his program for a just society, Prime Minister Trudeau proposed that civil servants should eventually have to be bilingual. This major effort has been opposed by several provincial premiers as "economically infeasible." The rise in the number and proportions of other ethnic groups, and their even greater tendency to be monolingual (the half-million Ukranians are an instance), raise some fears of multilinguistic Balkanization.[30]

Of representation in the bureaucracy it can be flatly noted that French Canadians have not been overevident. A 1958 study of the elite bureaucrats, the top 202 posts, found only 13.4 percent of them to be French Canadians. Even more significant is the fact that half of these were recruited late in life apparently to secure a "tactful" balance of nationalities:

There are various ways in which this imbalance of the two major ethnic components of the population can be interpreted. The low proportion of French Canadians would suggest that the demands for appointment on ethnic grounds

[29] *A Preliminary Report of the Royal Commission on Bilingualism and Biculturalism* (Ottawa: Queen's Printer, 1965).

[30] *New York Times*, January 26, 1964, p. 9; February 4, 1964, p. 26; February 21, 1964, p. 54; February 26, 1964, p. 46.

*per se* have been kept in check. Or conversely, the tendency to meet such demands by appointments from outside would suggest that ethnicity has been in some cases an over-riding consideration. It must be remembered, however, that French-Canadian education has not provided a large reservoir of administrators who could eventually be promoted to the higher levels. It is likely also that the motivation of French Canadians to serve the centralized state is not as great as that of English Canadians, although the limited opportunities for French Canadians to move up hierarchies in the private corporate world should make the bureaucracy an attractive alternative. It would appear, then, that as far as higher posts are concerned, the efficiency of the service has been as important as the promotion of national unity.[31]

John Porter, who compared his own sample of the business elite with that of the public service, concluded that the government service was more open on this factor than the business elite—as it was with respect to selection according to social class and religion. Yet his conclusion is as emphatic as his remedies are anticlimactic:

> The analysis of the social class and ethnic origins of the senior officials suggests that the bureaucracy is more closed than open. If the Canadian bureaucracy is to be brought closer to the ideal of rationalized, rivalled, and open, it will be necessary to develop more fully the bureaucratic career, particularly by reducing the number of outside appointments at high levels and thus making these senior positions the career goals that they should be. It is also important that the skills and knowledge of the highly trained should be distributed through other institutional structures so that criticism and alternative policies can be built on firmer ground. Policies of recruitment and promotion must seek the ability that lies at the lower levels of the bureaucratic hierarchy and the class system. It is not the bureaucracy alone that must change for it is geared into the institutional machinery of the wider society. The distribution of technical competency, for example, depends on the educational system.[32]

We have already questioned his characterization of national unity as irrational (Chapter 4, pp. 73-74). So too did Donald Rowat:

> I believe his acceptance of the Weberian typology as a normative ideal has caused him to lay too much stress on the desirability of neutrality and of the bureaucratic career as its prerequisite. He even goes so far as to say that "modern bureaucracies ideally require social eunuchs who have been neutralized as persons within their own societies and who have divested themselves of interests in social groups and institutions involved in the struggle for power" (p. 490). But surely there are degrees or stages of neutrality only some of which are

---

[31] John Porter, "Higher Public Servants and the Bureaucratic Elite in Canada," *The Canadian Journal of Economics and Political Science*, XXIV, November (1958), 491.

[32] Porter, "Higher Public Servants," p. 496.

desirable. . . . One of my fears about a civil service made up entirely of career bureaucrats is that it would lose contact with and lack understanding of the changing feelings, needs, and desires of the great variety of people and groups found in our dynamic, pluralistic society.[33]


## IV.  CONFESSIONAL BUREAUCRACIES: THE CASE OF LEBANON

Religion is historically another basis for profound social cleavage. It has also been a foundation of bureaucratic selectivity. The milder forms of selectivity consist of a pattern of allocation of a few offices, for example, the balance of a combined ethnic and religious ticket in New York City and New York State politics. More extensively a particular position may become religiously identified or allocated; examples are the traditional but not invariable designation of the Democratic National Chairman or the presidency of Hunter College as "Catholic" positions, and the Jewish Supreme Court Justice. Even more extensively an agency may become the preserve of a religion. Brian Chapman's authoritative interpretation of bureaucracies, *The Profession of Government*, speaks of such a pattern of control as "colonization" and describes the Ministry of Education in Belgium and the Ministry of Population in France as Catholic preserves. On the other hand, active Free Masonry is still a useful attribute in the French Ministry of the Interior.[34]

In Lebanon the process of careful quotas for all principal religions is carried out in intricate, loving detail. The general pattern emerges from the constitution promulgated May 23, 1926, and from practice developed under French hegemony in the 1930s and culminating in the National Pact of 1943 which fixes the basic pattern and compromise that allows this badly divided society to function in relatively stable fashion. As amended in 1943, Article 95 of the constitution provides that "as a provisional measure and for the sake of justice and amity, the communities (religious sects) shall be equitably represented in public employment and in the composition of the Ministry." At the highest level this arrangement is represented by the pattern of a Maronite—the largest group—as President, a Sunni Moslem as Prime Minister, while the President of the Chamber of Deputies is drawn from the sect of the Shi'ites. The lesser positions are allocated in accordance with elaborate sect and geographic rules.[35]

[33] Donald C. Rowat, "On John Porter's 'Bureaucratic Elite in Canada,'" *Canadian Journal of Economics and Political Science*, XXV, May (1959), 206–7.

[34] Brian Chapman, *The Profession of Government* (London: George Allen & Unwin, 1959), pp. 285–86.

[35] See Clyde G. Hess and Herbert Bodman, Jr., "Confessionalism and Feudality in Lebanese Politics," *Middle East Journal*, VIII, Winter (1954), 23 for a detailing of these rules.

The extent to which confessionalism—politics based on religion or sect—dominates Lebanese thinking is reflected in an anecdote that J. C. Hurewitz reports continued to circulate in Arab countries long after 1949:

> On the Lebanese front in the Palestine war of 1948 a Maronite Lieutenant found a Greek Catholic platoon in a state of complete inactivity despite the unabating and still vigorous exchange of fire. "Sergeant," bellowed the company commander, "don't your men know that this is war? Why aren't they fighting? If they do not take up their arms at once, I shall have you and them executed as deserters." "But one of our men was just killed, sir. We are therefore waiting for three Maronites, two Sunnis, two Shi'is, two Greek Orthodox, and one Druze also to be killed before we resume fighting." [36]

Since 1943 there has been no census for fear the changing population proportions will wreck the fragile settlement and agreement on new ratios would not be possible. The legislature has had to be constituted on multiples of eleven to allow a ratio of six Christians to five non-Christians, though the Moslems claim they are now the majority. Edward Shils captures the situation admirably:

> The working Constitution of the country is made rigid by the National Pact, which prevents the Chamber of Deputies from being a forum of real competition of ideas, and prevents the elections from being a real competition of parties. The party system is to a large extent a modern facade to the system of communities which lies behind it. The National Pact limits efficiency in the civil service by making communal membership a major criterion for recruitment. The government of the day is prevented from doing much at a time in the century when governments which are not "dynamic" are thought everywhere to be unworthy of continued existence.
>
> This paralysis of governmental action is a necessary condition for the avoidance of injury or the appearance or intention of injury to the interests of any one of the major communities. Even curiosity to know the truth about the confessional composition of the population must be kept in check in order to avoid the provocation of group rivalries and the anxieties which these would stimulate.[37]

The system is not by any means absolutely rigid. After the 1958 difficulties the cabinet was temporarily composed entirely of Maronites and Sunnis—the two contenders—in careful fashion. Ralph E. Crow also reports two unofficial studies of the distribution of major administrative positions that indicate considerable fluidity over time and something less than complete

[36] J. C. Hurewitz, "Lebanese Democracy in its International Setting," in *Politics in Lebanon*, ed. Leonard Binder (New York: John Wiley, 1966), p. 213.

[37] Edward Shils, "The Prospect for Lebanese Civility," in *Politics in Lebanon*, p. 4.

equity (see Table 5.4). While all figures—including the population figures—are somewhat disputable, the general configuration of overrepresentation of Shi'ites is confirmed by observers of the system.

**TABLE 5.4**    **Distribution of Higher Administrative Positions Among Religious Communities in 1946 and 1955**

|  | Maronite | Sunni | Shi'ite | Greek Orthodox | Greek Catholic | Druze | Total Number of Cases |
|---|---|---|---|---|---|---|---|
| Percent of posts, 1946 | 38.7 | 29 | 3.2 | 19.3 | 3.2 | 6.4 | 31 |
| Percent of posts, 1955 | 40.0 | 27 | 3.6 | 11.7 | 9.0 | 7.2 | 111 |
| Percent of population, 1956 | 30.0 | 20 | 18.0 | 10.0 | 6.0 | 6.0 | 1,430,908 |

Source: Taken from Halim Fayyad, *The Effects of Sectarianism in Lebanese Administration*, unpublished M.A. thesis, American University of Beirut, 1956, as printed in Ralph E. Crow, "Confessionalism, Public Administration, and Efficiency in Lebanon," in *Politics in Lebanon*, ed. Leonard Binder (New York: John Wiley, 1966), p. 172.

Sectarian conflict is exacerbated by strong family loyalties. In 1964, 17 families competed for Chamber seats in 22 of the 26 districts.[38] Because personal feuds become family feuds, the delicate art of balancing becomes even more intricate.

The growth of the bureaucracy has been rather rapid—from 6,000 in 1943 to more than 16,000 in 1960, according to Ralph E. Crow.[39] Control is made difficult by the tendency of ministers to function quite independently of the cabinet, thus adding to the complication of there being two heads of government, some of the characteristics of committeelike leadership. It is difficult, for example, to classify Lebanon as either a presidential or cabinet system, because the carefully articulated system balances communal power in the prerogatives of the various officials.

Confessionalism is clearly not merely a question of who occupies what office. The most significant questions of international politics have hinged in large measure upon religious affiliation. The basis of the National Pact was an agreement between President Bishara al-Khuri and Prime Minister Riyad al-Sulh that Lebanon would remain a nation independent of other Arab

[38] Michael W. Suleiman, "Elections in a Confessional Democracy," *Journal of Politics*, XXIX, February (1967), 125.

[39] Ralph E. Crow, "Confessionalism, Public Administration, and Efficiency in Lebanon," in *Politics in Lebanon*, p. 178.

countries though "with an Arab face" and that Christians would end their French and Western orientation.[40] President Chamoun's ambiguous attitude toward the Pact was one of the precipitating causes of the crisis of 1958. The Moslem groups have been significantly more oriented to pan-Arabic notions than the most potent single group, the Christian (Maronite) Lebanese. This in turn has involved the Moslem groups' divergent attitudes towards the efforts of Nasser to unite the region under Egyptian leadership, which would of course be Moslem-dominated; toward Russian influence in the Middle East; toward the basing of terrorists on Lebanese soil; and even toward the level of anti-Israeli activity in the 1967 war. Lebanon at that time took no role, and its whole attitude is one of scrupulous attention to its own borders and maintaining its own identity rather than sacrificing itself for any pan-Arab cause. The classic identification of its position is that no one knows which Middle-Eastern country will be the first to make peace with Israel but that everyone knows the second will be Lebanon. That is to say that its leaders are quite willing to take this step if they can do so without undue offense to the Moslem portion of the population.

Orientations to the West—France and England in the 1940s versus Pan-Arabism, or the United States or the Soviet Union in the 1950s—also follow confessional lines and become intertwined with them and patronage and position. The French have maintained considerable influence, particularly in education, where 40 percent of the children still learn French; the American University still cannot gain recognition for its bachelor's degree because of this orientation.[41] Not accidentally, perhaps, the Ministry of Education has been dominated by Christian, almost invariably Maronite, leadership.[42] President Chamoun's efforts for reelection became entangled with his pro-Western orientation and clan and sect rivalries. Similarly, the 1969 cabinet crisis revolved around Moslem orientations toward Nasser and the terrorists.

The strength of the country has been its modern attitude toward industry and commerce. As Shils notes:

> Lebanon, and perhaps Malaysia—the only new states having a vigorous, productive, and profitable economic life—are capable of providing employment outside the government for a considerable proportion of those who enter the labor market in the modern sector of its economy. Lebanon has the further advantage, which Malaysia lacks, that its business enterprisers are ethnically Arab (even though they might be Christians), and therefore ethnically homogeneous with the rest of Lebanon's population—unlike the Chinese

[40] Hess and Bodman, Jr., "Confessionalism and Feudality in Lebanese Politics," p. 24.
[41] *New York Times*, January 28, 1967, p. 3.
[42] Ralph Crow, "Religious Sectarianism in the Lebanese Political System," *Journal of Politics*, XXIV, 1962, Table 5, 506.

businessmen in Malaysia. This helps to make private business enterprise a morally legitimate activity in Lebanon. The civil servants and politicians do not despise it and no one has to curry public favor by abusing it. Most of the younger generation of educated middle-class persons do not, like their coevals in other countries in their part of the world, espouse antibourgeois attitudes to any great extent. Businessmen are able to carry on their activities in a congenial atmosphere. This situation contributes to their effectiveness and restrains a potential conflict which is much stronger in most other new states. It also means that the government is not driven to become very active in the economic sphere.[43]

Such modernity has not been as evident in its governmental service. Indeed as Shils notes the visibility of business has meant that society's best minds have not been drawn to government service. Efforts to modernize the bureaucracy have been thwarted by the peculiarities of Lebanese politics. Yet there is discussion and effort even to the point of considering modification of the communal emphasis. Efforts to rationalize and modernize within the limits imposed by reality seem to offer hope for continued social progress.

## V.  ETHNIC DIFFERENCES AND CONFESSIONAL INTEGRATION:  THE CASE OF ISRAEL

The modern Jewish state is largely a creature of the post-World War I era.[44] Its founding fathers are thus alive and in many cases well-entrenched in the party-dominated bureaucracy. Veneration for their achievement is sufficient for them to dismiss as presumptuous any proposals for compulsory retirement from parliament at age 70, and to perpetuate a situation where leaders in their fifties with decades of experience are regarded as promising youngsters.

Very strict party control lines reinforce traditional respect in a society dominated by political parties. It is possible to buy real estate, raise capital, and arrange for medical care outside these lines, but it is generally easier to do these things within them. This has particular significance with respect to the dominant Labor party and its controlling wing, the old MAPAI group, from whose ranks every prime minister, foreign minister, and finance minister in Israel's history have been drawn. MAPAI also controls the Histadrut, the central labor federation, which is in turn the country's largest employer and

---

[43] Edward Shils, "The Prospect of Lebanese Civility," in *Politics in Lebanon*, Leonard Binder (ed.), p. 6.

[44] For background see Eisenstadt, S.N. (ed.) *Integration and Development in Israel* (New York: Praeger, 1970); Alex Weingrad, *Israel: Group Relation in a New Society* (London: Pall Mall, 1965); Judith Shuval, *Immigrants on the Threshold* (New York: Atherton, 1963); Dorothy Willner, *Nation-Building and Community in Israel* (Princeton, N.J.: Princeton University Press, 1969).

source of nongovernmental investment capital. The Histadrut controls most of the construction industry for example. And the society is used to the principle of party representation in almost every aspect of life, and at least tolerates party patronage notions in most of them.

As successive waves of immigration have come to Israel the percentages of the electorate controlled by the parties have remained remarkably steady. The parties built on ideological differences—some originating in nuances of approaches to socialism as seen in turn-of-the-century Eastern Europe, and some built on the mix of illegal means to fight the British—have retained preeminence, while ethnic parties or regional ones have been conspicuously unsuccessful. Indeed, ethnic appeals are regarded as basically improper, as threatening to divide the society into two basic and potentially hostile "streams"—the dominant Central and Eastern European "veteran" community and the new majority of settlers from countries with Arab cultures (Iraq, Yemen, Morocco, and Algeria). The task of socializing these largely postindependence settlers was actually allocated in rough proportion to party strength as was the function of finding them niches in society, so that each party was able to establish links with the new groups even as they came off the ships and planes. The success of these and other efforts are seen in the stability of parties in these decades. The religious parties are somewhat stronger—orthodoxy is firmly in the "oriental" tradition. The Herut wing of the middle-class GAHAL party is somewhat strengthened, for its Irredentist tinge has somewhat greater appeal to the new immigrants who, as refugees from Arab countries, are quite hostile because of their treatment there. The MAPAM's militant Marxism has little consonance with the more concrete, less abstract thought patterns and Kibbutz practice, so their ideology has not attracted the "Sephardim" or "orientals." But these changes are minor and probably not unique even to these social groups. MAPAM has also suffered from a pro-Soviet stance.

In consequence, rather rigid patterns of promotion and control are evident in the public and semipublic bureaucracies, with low turnover rates and high degrees of party intervention; power in the party is itself based in large part on seniority and painfully acquired power over time.

To effect greater opportunity under this heavily establishment-, continuity-oriented system, direct measures were called for. The solution has been direct recruiting with differential grade and test scores required from individuals of different cultural backgrounds. Certain ministries have been the particular preserves of the orientals, for example, the post office, and it and others have been assigned to the religious parties for political rather than ethnic reasons. The oriental leadership has been largely, although not exclusively, concentrated in relatively routine, noncreative positions. Grumbling on this point has tended to be subsumed in the general generational discontent with leadership turnover, and in the more diffuse dissatisfactions with the general status of orientals in Israeli society. At the municipal and other local levels, however, breakthroughs in political leadership and thereby into various public offices have occurred. The 1970s have also seen the emergence of a group of self-styled "Black Panthers" and occasional rioting. Group tensions tend to be negatively correlated with external pressures. The reality of outside danger serves to keep the issue from being pressed vigorously internally, while visible but not always effective processes of cooptation are the price the western establishment must pay to keep things under control.

The effect of these official and pragmatic efforts is that sephardim are being brought into policy-making positions, although at a relatively slow pace. Whether this is at a rate sufficient to avoid internal strife is problematic. In the interim the obvious external threat to survival provides a deterrant to the raising of divisive issues, while a common religious ethos and some measure of accommodation offer more positive inducements.

Israel remains most interesting because its internal problem in the long run is that of assimilating a majority into a dominant minority culture. It has a number of distinct advantages over societies dealing with the same problem, most notably the deeply felt emotional bond of religion (even for the atheist) and the conjoint sense of creation and survival under duress and threat of extermination. It also has a unique sense of conscious development and faith in social engineering. These should combine to make it a unique laboratory for intergroup harmonization—an issue which both current problems and history reflected in cultural memories make salient for Israeli society.

## VI.   SUMMARY AND CONCLUSIONS

The patterns described here are characteristic of troubled bureaucratic structures and societies with varying degrees of strain. The bureaucratic struggle closely mirrors social tension in almost every instance. It is rare for a bureaucratic structure to attempt to resolve a problem of social antagonism by excluding a group; more typically, the degree of inclusion and acceptance resembles that pattern seen in a society as a whole.

In a number of instances the bureaucracy attempts to further resolution of a social conflict through active intervention. It is more likely to be helpful if it is not merely a promoter of resolution but also part of the resolution. That is to say, an administrative effort to realign relationships is more likely to succeed if the bureaucracy bears some of the costs rather than merely shifting them to others.

# 6

# The American Bureaucracy as a Representational Service

## I. INTRODUCTION

The implicit assumption of Kingsley's *Representative Bureaucracy* (1944) was that the American civil service was just that—representative. As an American writer interested in public personnel selection, he found equity and efficiency in the merit system. It is a bit ironic to hear this student of Harold Laski praising an American structure at the expense of its British counterpart. Such praise was not at all characteristic of Laski's writing; in fact, the vast bulk of Anglo-American comparisons have almost uniformly extolled the English structures. In any event, this notion that the American bureaucracy has achieved representativeness may seem strange in an era which sees repeated changes in our organizations generally and, especially, our governmental structures called examples of congealed, submerged, "institutional bias." The truth is perhaps somewhere in between; assuredly it is more complex. The present chapter is an inventory of the historical and contemporary record, an attempt to weigh the old clichés of perfection against today's trite charges of inequity.

The very existence of several agencies whose job is to eliminate discrimination, the constant announcements of new successes, all constitute what lawyer's call a "confession in avoidance." Throughout the federal bureaucracy we are constantly told in effect that such things happened previously, but not now. Each new administrator speaks of his predecessors in that way, and many successors, we suspect, will subsequently say the same things about the present incumbents.

Unmistakably the Russians have sought out women astronauts where we have not. Our elite structures—the Foreign Service, the astronaut program, the FBI, the regulatory commissions—remain "waspy" male strongholds, as we are too often waspishly reminded. To date the presidency has been held exclusively by individuals of Western European descent. While women have been prime ministers in "developing" nations like India, Ceylon, and Israel, and political leaders in their own right in older systems like England's, they have not by 1972 received an appointment to the Supreme Court or any but token appointments to high administrative posts in the United States.

But what does this do to the picture created by Kingsley? Is there no truth to the older dream of the equitable merit system or is it, as "Nader's raiders" suggested in a recent study, a "spoiled system" immersed in inequity? A study of the attitudes of federal employees showed many negative as well as positive evaluations of the service were made; for example, a sense of frustration and encrusted immobility existed among some employees. But there was also a strong sense that the federal service was a better employer than could be found in the private sector.

Is this an illusion, a myth, the product of past slogans? By and large employees are rational evaluators of their employer, their working conditions, and their market alternatives. Might the most important evaluation perhaps be theirs and not ours?

The answers to these questions rest in part upon comparisons with other employers within the society and with other bureaucracies in other societies. It is not just the performance of the American civil service in absolute terms, but the performances of other agencies that also help characterize the degree of civil service effectiveness. Finally, expectations (often influenced by the operations of other structures) influence perception as well. Thus relative performance is an issue that must also be examined.

There is a final area of concern: the goals for the future development of representativeness in the American bureaucracies, and the means to be adopted for their implementation. The goal of increasing representativeness is clear, while the means have been gradually altering. Although it had not (at this writing) accepted quotas as direct limitations, the Civil Service

**TABLE 6.1**      **Four Social Characteristics of General Federal Employees and the General Employed
Public**

| Social Characteristic | General Federal Employees (N = 948) | General Employed Public (1,142) |
|---|---|---|
| Religious Preference: | | |
| Protestant | 61% | 69% |
| Catholic | 31 | 25 |
| Jewish | 5 | 4 |
| Other or none | 4 | 2 |
| Race: | | |
| White | 79 | 89 |
| Nonwhite | 21 | 11 |
| Age: | | |
| Under 20 | 0 | 2 |
| 20–24 | 3 | 8 |
| 25–34 | 18 | 22 |
| 35–44 | 37 | 29 |
| 45–54 | 27 | 25 |
| 55 and over | 15 | 13 |
| Identification: | | |
| Democrat | 55 | 48 |
| Republican | 17 | 26 |
| Independent | 23 | 17 |
| No choice | 5 | 9 |

Reprinted from Milton C. Cummings, Jr., M. Kent
Jennings, and Franklin P. Kilpatrick, "Federal and Nonfederal Employees: A Comparative Social-Occupational
Analysis," *Public Administration Review*, Vol. 27, December
1967, p. 399.

Commission had asked each unit to establish "goals." This also creates an
incentive to hire "qualifiable" (but perhaps less qualified) individuals for
most positions. Whether this will prove effective, and be accepted as
legitimate, or whether it will prove destructive and divisive is a question that
will also be addressed here.

## II.  THE HISTORY OF THE SERVICE

The American public service inherited the tradition of the unrecon-
structed, patronage-ridden British civil service of the eighteenth century. The
casual, somewhat antiefficient operation described with brilliance and insight
in Leonard White's *The Federalists*[1] (a history of our administrative beginnings) would not be totally unfamiliar to the reader of Dickens's *Bleak House*.[2]
Certainly among the dominant principles in selection were the old
regime's notions of family and patronage. These notions were hampered only
slightly by the absence of a well-established aristocracy. Thus, in 1804 the
Livingstone-Clinton family had, it is calculated, sixteen positions in government that produced a total income of $60,500.[3] Journalists who vigorously,
sometimes vituperatively, supported one or another political faction—people
like Tench Coxe, Jefferson's propagandist—were also favorite recipients of
patronage.
With respect to theories of public employment, the Jeffersonian and
Jacksonian movements can best be understood as efforts to abort any notion
of public office as a hereditary right. The challenge to the Federalist claims of
control by the best families and the rights of entrenched officeholders was in
part the obvious predestined role of the outs against the ins, but it also seems
to have reflected genuine ideological differences. In these matters, one can
emphasize the continuity with past practice or the change that occurred
pretty much as one chooses. Viewed from on high, chronologically, and in an
even deeper sense, history is a seamless web: "No man writes on a clean
slate." In another sense, every event is unique with its incredible richness and
potentiality for emergent outcomes. White's histories of American administration set forth the clearly evolving, continuous dependency of the Jeffersonians and Jacksonians upon the basic administrative foundations laid by the
Federalists, whose enduring contribution is emphasized. Yet, in selection of
personnel and in attitude toward office, there were demonstrable changes.
And if we accept the conclusions of Sidney Aronson in his freshly conceived
volume entitled *Status and Kinship in the Higher Civil Service*,[4] it was the
Jeffersonians with their quieter formulas who nonetheless made the significant breakthrough. Though they did not develop exciting slogans, they
accomplished more of their goals.
It was an avowed aim of Jefferson to end the monopoly of key positions

---

[1] Leonard White, *The Federalists* (New York: Macmillan, 1948).

[2] Charles Dickens, *Bleak House* (London: Bradbury & Evans, 1853).

[3] Carl Russell Fish, *The Civil Service and the Patronage* (New York: Longmans, Green, 1905),
p. 87.

[4] See Sidney Aronson, *Status and Kinship in the Higher Civil Service* (Cambridge, Mass.:
Harvard University Press, 1964).

carefully fostered by the Federalists—especially the Hamiltonians—even at the expense of Adams's followers. "Is it political intolerance to claim a proportionate share in the direction of the public affairs?" queried the sage of Monticello, a man who understood as well as Hamilton, and much better than Adams, the uses of patronage and the art of political leverage, the arcane potentialities of influence. Against a claim to power based on the emphemeral support of mere majorities, the Federalists clung to their notion of property in office and to a thinly veiled claim of an inherent right to rule. They thus played directly into the hands of their opponents and blundered into oblivion. Veterans of wars and long-time public officials had an "implicit contract," one which entitled them "to spend the evening of their days in ease and competence," [5] wrote journalist William Coleman, probably at the instigation of Alexander Hamilton.

While the Jeffersonians were effective at least in part in rejecting Coleman's plea and other similar arguments, the Jacksonians made that rejection one of their major slogans. Richard Hofstadter has suggested there was more bluster than reality to Jackson's militant leveling; we can paraphrase by suggesting that Jackson was the unconscious prototype of Harrison's conscious demagoguery. At any rate, the thundering absolute of William Marcy's "to the victor belong the spoils" obscures much more modest actions. We are assured by Erik M. Eriksson that the turnover did not exceed 10 to 20 percent of the service.[6] According to Aronson, the social composition of the administration of this patron and ally of the locofocos— the supposedly radical wing of the party—was a shade more aristocratic than under Jefferson.

The victory of the Jacksonians fixed the mold of discussion of public office. Rotation in office of all officials and the eligibility of all citizens for any office became an integral part of the democratic credo. The glorification of the common yeoman was made an article of faith, precisely as his day was declining.

Civil-service reform was the goal and the apothesis of the middle class. As in England, the push came from those dissatisfied with abuses rather than in the name of egalitarianism. Highly moralistic slogans of efficiency and honesty were invoked by the educated who wished to substitute performance standards as an alternative to upper-class preference or mass power. The "boss" and the "machine" were to be replaced by scientific selection. The new methods would above all lead to an honest service and hopefully a cheap one. Objective selection would lead to objective conduct. To counter opposition to civil-service reform which invoked the image of a privileged

[5] Fish, *The Civil Service and the Patronage*, pp. 35–37.
[6] Erik M. Eriksson, "The Federal Civil Service under President Jackson," *Mississippi Valley Historical Review*, XIII, March (1927), 540.

class, a permanent aristocracy entrenched in their career positions, neither selected by nor responsive to public opinion, the reformers interposed the even more ominous picture of the undemocratic, nefarious boss.

The legal and structural foundations of the American civil service were laid in the 1880s. But the real growth and social character of the service are a post–World War I, 1930s, and World War II phenomenon. Both in size and direction, radical changes were experienced then which capped and consummated smaller, less obvious evolvements. These major quantum jumps are reflected in figures for both employment (see Table 6.2) and expenditures, and in terms of both the total picture and the patterning of expenditures.

**TABLE 6.2     The Growth of the Federal Service**

| Year | Number of employees |
|------|--------------------|
| 1816 | 4,837 |
| 1821 | 6,914 |
| 1861 | 36,672 |
| 1871 | 51,020 |
| 1881 | 100,020 |
| 1891 | 157,442 |
| 1908 | 356,753 |
| 1928 | 560,772 |
| 1938 | 882,226 |
| 1948 | 2,071,009 |
| 1957 | 2,417,565 |
| 1968 | 3,049,190 |

Sources: *Historical Statistics of the United States* (Washington, D.C.: Government Printing Office, 1961), pp. 710–11; and *Challenge and Change*, U.S. Civil Service Commission, Annual Report 1968 (Washington, D.C.: Government Printing Office, 1968), pp. 56–59.

For caveats on the accuracy of early figures see Paul Van Riper, *History of the U.S. Civil Service* (Evanston, Ill.: Row, Peterson, 1958), pp. 56–59.

These changes and their secular trends have many profound implications for government and society, only a few of which can be listed below:

1. The significance of government as an employer has been immensely

enhanced. One in six paychecks is governmental; some 4 percent are directly federal, while a considerable fraction of the remainder are indirectly supported.

2. The range of issues managed by bureaucracies is immensely greater, and the impact of their services on the daily lives of citizens is much greater. Post Office expenditures grew at an amount equal to one-third the total federal expenditures, or one-quarter the rate of welfare and related functions, during the first half of the twentieth century.[7] Personnel growth rates were even more dramatic.[8] The matters decided by the civil servant have greater relevance and affect more people in more ways than they did a century ago.

3. Announcement of a competitive, open system establishes norms and expectations whose violation is more visible and objectionable, more obvious and more grating. Failure to obtain or hold a position is associated, at least at face value, with incompetence or malfeasance, rather than (let us say) with not having the proper connections and/or with having supported the wrong candidate. Deviations from such an idealized system will be more objectionable because of the stigma involved in nonemployment.

4. The multiplication of functions usually carries with it increasing opportunity for different specializations, functional types, and personality types.

5. The development of a service-oriented bureaucracy requires more social interpretation by the bureaucracy; opportunities for local, non-Washington employment increases with some localism making itself felt. The need for effective public relations is underscored and growth in this direction can also emphasize representational responsibilities. (On the other hand, large units also contribute an aura of Machiavellian maneuver, of mass manipulation by a crafty autocrat.)

## III.  EQUAL EMPLOYMENT, MINORITIES, AND DISCRIMINATION

"Let's face it, the merit system was set up in the 1880's by white men for white men, not for Negroes or for women," observes Evelyn Harrison, Deputy Director of the Bureau of Policies and Standards, in the Civil Service Commission's Annual Report for 1968.[9]

Paul Van Riper's history of the United States civil service is predicated on the assumption that:

*There is not now, nor has there been in the United States since the early days of the constitution, any small privileged class which could block legislation in the manner in which it has*

[7] Solomon Fabricant, *The Trend of Government Activity in the United States Since 1900* (New York: National Bureau of Economic Research, 1952), pp. 176–79 and 182–84.

[8] Fabricant, *The Trend of Government Activity*, p. 186.

[9] *Challenge and Change*, United States Civil Service Commission Annual Report, 1968 (Washington, D.C.: Government Printing Office, 1968), p. 21.

*frequently been stopped during periods of English history. There have been fewer barriers between mass desire and governmental action in the United States than in most countries.*[10] (Italics mine.)

This may be true in terms of any tight social class control in the sense of, say, Mills's power elite, yet the dominant tone of civil service reform was, as we have often remarked, middle class. The reformers were moralists—hence the epithet "snivel service"—who wanted to elevate equity. But the evils they saw were from political influence which arbitrarily affected selection. Only over time were regulations affecting other forms of favoritism or particularistic selection and promotion gradually examined and dealt with. Discrimination in selection by religion was also prohibited early. However, no explicit prohibition of discrimination in promotion was on the books.

Discrimination by race was outlawed by executive regulation in November, 1940, and by law—the Ramspeck Act—nineteen days later. In fact, the Executive Order was rushed through under threat of a congressman —a Southerner at that—appearing more zealous in securing Negro rights than the Roosevelt New Deal administration.[11] Effective implementation, however, was extremely deliberate. Desegregation of the armed forces and a weak Fair Employment Commission came as a result of a threat by A. Philip Randolph to lead a wartime march on Washington. President Truman's administration made significant though small efforts, and the Eisenhower years saw the basic machinery established. But a concentrated, head-on, and effective campaign had to wait until well into the Kennedy administration, when something moral, or political, or both inspired the Kennedy brothers to move from amorphous sympathy into effective action. The key event may have been a conversation between Robert Kennedy, then Attorney General, and Atlanta businessmen during which his appeals for employment of Blacks were met by unfavorable, and accurate, contrasts of the employment records of local federal agencies in this area as compared to the private sector. Lyndon Johnson's administration was also aggressive as befitted the new power of the man who had headed the President's Committee on Equal Employment Opportunity during its most successful years.

The results have been superficially most impressive. The most comprehensive sampling of civil servants found a surprisingly large component of nonwhites (21 percent) as early as 1964. Mass head counts over the years by the Civil Service Commission are more conservative, and although the difficulties involved in superiors having to attribute minority group status are great, the Commission's counts are probably closer to reality. Nonetheless, it is clear that Blacks have for some years now been employed dispropor-

[10] Paul Van Riper, *History of the United States Civil Service* (Evanston, Ill.: Row Peterson & Co., 1958), p. 4.
[11] Van Riper, *History of the United States Civil Service*, pp. 155–56n.

tionately in federal service and have been convinced—almost certainly correctly—that Uncle Sam is among the best *equal* employment opportunity employers. In 1972, Negroes constituted 15 percent of all federal employees, and 11.3 percent of those in the civil service. Approximately 93,000 more positions were being held by Blacks than in 1962, representing better than one-third of the total increase of the entire service during that decade. Table 6.3 presents data showing the improvement in level of Negro employment in the decade 1962 to 1971. Two things, however, should also be noted. First, the rate of increase of minority employment in state and local government has far outstripped the federal increase—and probably with less diligent effort. This suggests the possibility that federal government employment may be less attractive in a full-employment economy and that minority employment increases may result from economic necessity as much as from the new application of equity. Second, the bulk of the numerical improvement still involves low-level positions. The percentage increases at high GS levels are high but the increases in absolute numbers though solid are slim. (An increase from one to two after all represents 100 percent improvement.)

A derivative of the concentration on Negro officeholding has been a relatively new emphasis on Mexican-American, Indian, Oriental, Eskimo, and Aleuts recruitment and promotion in the civil service.

The number of Spanish-surnamed employees in the civil service has grown from less than 51,000 in 1962 to over 75,000 in 1971. In part this may be an artificial result of the change in classification from "Spanish speaking" to "Spanish surnamed" and better counting procedures. A clear actual increase of about 6,000 took place between 1967 and 1971. These represent unusually high gains under stringent conditions sometimes involving a decline of total positions in the service; from a situation in which they constituted 2.2 percent in 1963, they moved to constitute 2.9 percent of all employees in 1971. Civil-service improvement was comparable—from 1.4 percent in 1963 to 2.0 percent in 1971.

During the very brief period in which data has been separately kept, improvement in the numbers of other minorities employed has been small but clear. Improvement in levels of position has also been evident. By November, 1971, minority-group employees occupied 19.4 percent of all federal positions: 15.0 percent Black, 2.9 percent Spanish surname, 0.7 percent American Indian, and 0.8 percent Oriental American. These figures are higher than both the census proportion of these groups and their share of the labor force (black women are greatly overrepresented in the labor force). Their participation in the upper reaches of the bureaucracy, although geometric gains have been made since 1962, is still a small fraction of their porportion in the general population.

**TABLE 6.3    Improvement in Level of Negro Federal Civil Service Employment (1962–1971)**

| | June, 1962 | | | November, 1968 | | | November, 1971 | | |
|---|---|---|---|---|---|---|---|---|---|
| | Negro employees | % of all employees at this level | % of all Negro employees | Negro employees | % of all employees at this level | % of all Negro employees | Negro employees | % of all employees at this level | % of all Negro employees |
| GS 1–4 | 64,651 | 19.3 | 60.7 | 75,846 | 20.5 | 56.8 | 63,833 | 21.8 | 42.9 |
| 5–8 | 29,897 | 9.6 | 28.1 | 40,494 | 11.6 | 30.4 | 58,024 | 14.9 | 39.0 |
| 9–11 | 9,090 | 3.4 | 8.5 | 12,631 | 4.3 | 9.5 | 18,262 | 5.7 | 12.3 |
| 13–18 | 2,818 | 1.3 | 2.7 | 4,655 | 1.8 | 3.4 | 8,838 | 2.9 | 5.9 |
| Total | 106,456 | 13.5 | 100.0 | 133,626 | 14.9 | 100.0 | 148,957 | 15.0 | 100.0 |

Sources: *Study of Minority-Group Employment in the Federal Government* (Washington, D.C.: Government Printing Office, 1965 and 1972) and *Challenge and Change*, U.S. CSC Annual Report (Washington, D.C.: Government Printing Office, 1968), p. 77. Because of rounding, figures do not always equal 100%.

## Women in the Federal Service

A woman served as a postmaster—or is it postmistress?—as early as 1773, so that in one sense the federal service is antedated by feminine employment. The outstanding facts, however, are lack of female proportionality in the federal service—though representative of disproportionate participation in the job market—and the lack of higher level posts.[12]

There were isolated examples of women employees throughout the nineteenth century, particularly as small-town postmasters.[13] Clara Barton, for example, was employed as early as 1854 in the Patent Office. (During the Civil War she paid a substitute, while she went to the front. The concept of property in office made this practice of sending substitutes quite common.) However, the employment of women was not widespread until the Treasury Department began extensive use of "female clerks" in the 1860s. Legislation permitting such employment at $600 per year, about half the rate for males, was passed in 1864. An 1870 statute authorized agency heads to appoint women to higher clerkships at the same pay as men. This was interpreted to mean that executives could request applicants and fill most positions, utilizing sex as a criterion. Most executives followed this practice particularly at higher levels. In 1962 at the request of the President's Commission on the Status of Women, the Attorney General declared such an interpretation improper and in 1965 Congress repealed the statute to avoid any possibility of confusion.

With the passage of the Pendleton Act (1883), establishing the Civil Service, women were presumptively equal in the eyes of the Service. A woman made the highest score in the first (1883) Civil Service exam held in Washington and received the second appointment. The spread of the use of the typewriter coincided nicely with the introduction of Civil Service. The number of women employed grew rapidly, since it was assumed they were "naturally" more adept at use of the machine. With their increase came resistance to differential pay; in 1923 the Classification Act established the principle of payment by position and role and eliminated any sex differential in compensation.

Subsequently, on October 13, 1967, President Johnson signed Executive Order 11375 prohibiting discrimination against women in the federal service. Reinforcing the program of the previously established Interdepartmental Committee on the Status of Women, it also established procedures similar to those used by racial and other minorities for appeals against alleged

---

[12] "Study of Employment of Women in the Federal Government," United States Civil Service Commission, Statistics Section (Washington, D.C.: Government Printing Office, 1967).

[13] See Lucille Foster McMillin, *Women in the Federal Service*, United States Civil Service Commission (Washington, D.C.: Government Printing Office, 1938).

infractions.[14] In 1969, President Nixon by Executive Order 11478 incorporated the program into the Federal Equal Employment Opportunity program under the Civil Service Commission.

If we analyze the effects reported, some conclusions emerge that are perhaps surprising. Women represented 34.1 percent of all Civil Service employees on October 31, 1967, quite a bit below the 36.2 percent of the general employed labor force at that same time.[15] The percentage of women in the federal service has slowly gone down further during the years of the program from 34.1 percent in 1967 to 33.4 percent in 1969 and 33.2 percent in 1970. This represents an increase of less than 50,000 while the federal service increased by over 140,000. In 1969 to 1970 when the service decreased by 8,000, so did the number of women employees.

The male-female difference is most striking in the distribution by sex among the levels of position. Even with significant improvement in recent years, the differences emerge from even the simplest tabulations, as noted in Table 6.4.

**TABLE 6.4    Distribution Among Grades for Men and Women in the Federal Service**

| Grade | Men (in %) 1967 | Men (in %) 1970 | Women (in %) 1959 | Women (in %) 1967 | Women (in %) 1970 |
|---|---|---|---|---|---|
| 1–5 | 42 | 39.2 | 79 | 74 | 67.1 |
| 6–12 | 46 | 46.9 | 20 | 25 | 31.8 |
| 13–18 | 12 | 14.8 | below 0.5 | 1 | 1.2 |

Source: "Study of Employment of Women in the Federal Government," United States Civil Service Commission, 1967 and 1970 (Washington, D.C.: Government Printing Office), 1967, p. 1, and 1970, p. 17.

We have already noted the substantial absolute and relative increases in the numbers of higher-level positions held by women. President Johnson appointed 120 women to top-level positions in a period of less than two years. Women appointed as a result of taking the middle-management federal service Entrance Examination increased from 15 percent in 1961 to 33 percent in 1967.

A study by M. C. Cummings et al. indicated that women who worked for the government believed the Service more favorably inclined to women than private industry.[16] Women in private employment claimed no dif-

[14] *Challenge and Change*, p. 20.
[15] "Study of Employment," 1967.
[16] See Milton C. Cummings, M. K. Jennings, and Franklin P. Kilpatrick, "Federal and Nonfederal Employees: A Comparative Social-Occupational Analysis," *Public Administration*

ference. As with many attitude surveys it is difficult to disentangle cause and effect here.

## Preference:   Veterans and the Handicapped

Veterans' compensation has a long history, including the warrior's bounty and right to pillage. As early as the postrevolutionary period, war service was rewarded by giving parcels of land to former soldiers. Eighteen years before the Pendleton Act, in 1865, Congress enacted Veterans' Preference, which thus effectively antedates any merit system. Today, while veterans constitute 13 percent of the population and 30 percent of the labor force, they number some 51 percent of federal civilian employees.[17]

Preference for the handicapped is also indicated in somewhat weak form in legislation and regulations. This does not take the form of specific advantages or of regulations that can be invoked, but is rather more facilitative than regulative. In 1909 Theodore Roosevelt directed all agencies to provide the Commission with lists of positions that could be filled by deaf-mutes. Congress has provided preference for purchase of certain goods made by the blind. The Commission has also pressed for aid to the mentally retarded in the form of positions they can fill. In four years, they placed over 5,000.[18]

To some personnel officers and others, such an emphasis is the antithesis of civil service. These programs emphasize the need for recruitment based upon grounds Professor Porter assured us were worse than irrational—even unworthy. Whether a merit system should attempt to go beyond sorting out the qualified seems problematic. For others it has loomed as a creative opportunity giving purpose, direction, and even nobility to an otherwise routine and somewhat trivial function. The challenge of creative recruitment —"affirmative action" to create positive conditions for wider participation of groups—has a strong appeal. It presents a further dialectical challenge—to achieve all this without dilution of standards. The Civil Service Commission's 1968 Report has a touch of near eloquence (rare in government reports) on just this point:

> The charge is sometimes made that a sort of reverse discrimination is being
> practiced to the detriment of the merit system. As we keep trying to make clear
> to our own people and to the agencies we serve, the program is intended to
> remove racist barriers which have kept competent men and women out of

*Review*, XXVII, December (1967). Incidentally, a USCSC survey found women did not prefer male to female supervisors. While men did, they were less likely to do so if they had had experience with a woman supervisor.

[17] *Challenge and Change*, p. 23.
[18] *Challenge and Change*, p. 22.

Government. It is not intended to reduce the standards of Federal employment to let the incompetent into Government.

In our efforts to put opportunity within the reach of all, we have run into still another problem which should be frankly faced. We have seen the growth of what might be called "the tyranny of color." An incompetent manages to hold onto his job only because of his race. This form of blackmail cannot be tolerated. Equal opportunity to be hired implies an equal opportunity to be fired. Jackie Robinson broke the color line in major league baseball not on the day he first took the field for the Brooklyn Dodgers but on the day he was first booed by the fans. Not until then did they accept him as a player rather than a social experiment.[19]

Reassessment of the purpose and validity of examining procedures has an intellectual excitement of its own. Continued emphasis on upgrading of skills has brought to many personnel officers a sense of personal achievement often lacking in such posts. If the great weakness of organization is lethargy, then this experiment may be a significant offset to any costs. The surprisingly high consequences of veterans' preference belies the purity of objections to other programs, which may look like greater paper concessions but which involve rather smaller numbers in actual operations.

## IV.  OTHER CHARACTERISTICS AND TRENDS

In 1903, about 62 percent of all federal employees and 60 percent of all civil servants were in the Post Office (see Table 6.5). Today that agency, though grown fourfold, constitutes less than one-fourth of the federal service. That simple fact alone suggests the shift from relatively routine to more demanding functions. It is difficult to get precisely comparable figures for the growths of differing functions, but in 1951 the Bureau of Labor Statistics made a comparison of selected groups and their growth during the period 1938 to 1951 when the total civilian labor force increased by about 100 percent.[20] While the rate of growth of clerical help over the period exceeded that of the more professional groups, the growth toward the end of the period reflected greater demands for professional skills. The sampling in 1951 found that United States government engineers and physicists constitute about one-eighth of all engineers employed in the country and one-fifth of all physicists, well beyond the expected ratios.

Pronounced differences between the general employed public and bureaucracy are also evident.[21] We have already discussed some of these

[19] *Challenge and Change*, p. 18.

[20] Bureau of Labor Statistics, *Federal White-Collar Workers*, Bull. 1117 (Washington, D.C.: Government Printing Office, June, 1951), p. 3.

[21] Cummings et al., "Federal and Nonfederal Employees," pp. 395 and 398.

**TABLE 6.5     Distribution of Employment by Agency (in %),
1903–1968**

| Department | 1968 All | 1903 All | 1903 Civil Service |
|---|---|---|---|
| Defense (1903, War & Navy) | 43.5 | 20.5 | 8.5 |
| Post Office | 24.2 | 62.3 | 59.8 |
| Veterans' Administration | 5.8 | — | — |
| Agriculture | 4.0 | 1.5 | 2.7 |
| Health-Education-Welfare | 3.9 | — | — |
| Treasury | 3.0 | 8.7 | 15.3 |
| Interior | 2.6 | 4.1 | 5.6 |
| Transport | 2.1 | — | — |
| State | 1.6 | 0.1 | 0.1 |
| GSA | 1.3 | — | — |
| Labor (1903, Commerce and Labor) | 1.2 | 2.4 | 4.3 |
| Justice | 1.2 | .3 | .5 |
| NASA | 1.1 | — | — |
| Other agencies | 4.5 | .1 | 3.1 |

Source: Derived from *The Executive Civil Service of the United States* (Washington, D.C.: Government Printing Office, 1904), pp. 9–10 and *Challenge and Change*, U.S. Civil Service Commission, Annual Report 1968 (Washington, D.C.: Government Printing Office, 1968), pp. 66–67.

differences in Chapter 3 and on page 106 of this chapter.

Projections by the Civil Service Commission suggest that for the next few years there will be above-average growth in professional occupations (especially economists, electronic engineers, and in education) and especially large increases in middle-skill jobs (social insurance claims and tax accounting).[22] The mix of positions will remain about the same though lower-graded occupations will grow a trace more rapidly (8.6 percent growth compared to 7.3 percent).

Today's federal civil servants are more likely to have grown up in an urban rather than a rural setting and are less likely to have come from a farm family than the general population; otherwise, they closely approximate the general populace. They are also slightly more likely to be first-generation Americans than the general populace. W. Lloyd Warner's study of federal executives found little difference between his group and business executives and concluded there was little to support the notion that government service

[22] United States Civil Service Commission, *Federal Work Force Outlook* (Washington, D.C.: Government Printing Office, March, 1968), pp. 8–9.

was a better vehicle for rising in the social structure.[23] Cummings et al. suggest that federal civil servants are much more likely to have had parents in public administration and to have another member of the family so employed. This must be qualified by Warner's finding that this former quality appears to reflect a general middle-class predisposition; that is, business executives also have parents with public administration backgrounds in roughly the same numbers. Nonetheless Cummings et al. conclude:

> In general, then, there is some evidence of predisposing effects in the home, operating on preadults and adults, which encourage persons to enter public versus nonpublic employment. The choice of public employment among our federal respondents is certainly greater than would be expected by chance. In addition to myriad other factors determining specific choice of employer, the direct and indirect cues transmitted in the home would seem to result in some differential selection of public employment.[24]

This somewhat generalized picture must be qualified by at least some notes as to specific structures. Gross figures can conceal odd differentials. (One is reminded of the mythical business where the owner earned a million dollars per year while his employee earned one dollar; together they had an average income of $500,000.50.)

The representativeness of the totality is rather belied in several particulars. Most obvious are regional differences with respect to the representativeness of minority groups in the South and Southwest. Employment of women shows regional variability as well.

## V. SPECIFIC AGENCIES AND REPRESENTATIVENESS

Agencies obviously have varied patterns. The Department of Agriculture, known to some as the "last refuge of the confederacy," has generally maintained a surprising conservatism of policy relating to personnel even under a host of celebrated "liberal" Secretaries of Agriculture. Its racial practices with respect to both employees and clientele groups have been laggard as compared to most major departments. The Patent Office (as noted earlier in this chapter) and the Department of Treasury were early employers of women. Selective policies may indeed be reflected in branches of the same agency. Secretary of the Interior Harold Ickes pioneered in nonsegregated services in the South and high-level Negro appointments, but the Forest Service in his department retained a rather puristic Brahminism.

[23] W. Lloyd Warner *et al.*, *The American Federal Executive* (New Haven, Conn.: Yale University Press, 1963).

[24] Cummings et al., "Federal and Nonfederal Employees," p. 396.

Among all agencies, the State Department has been the most significant one to attract charges of similar restrictiveness. Evidence has been accumulated to substantiate this in many ways. The department was until very recently very stuffy about hiring women. Underrepresentation of all standard minorities—racial and religious—has been pronounced. A near-monopoly by Eastern-establishment college graduates has been alleged and although this has been shown to be exaggerated, some of this indictment has bite. Van Riper speaks of the State Department as the one agency flatly having been class-dominated. His optimism that the Wriston Report of 1954 marked the end of such upper-class bias has been only partly justified. James McCamy's studies certainly indicate considerable openness of the system, but the response of the whole has been disappointing.[25]

Perhaps the strongest charge against the State Department has been the dominance in it of classicist, area-study thinking in determining policy. The Wriston suggestions were expected to introduce a new era where economists, labor specialists, and other specialists would share in decision-making. The hope was that this would have a general salutary effect, with fresh orientations in a stuffy institution. But the traditionalists have rather effectively prevailed within the department, thwarting several Presidents and Secretaries of State. But Presidents have a way of getting revenge even on major institutions. Gradually growing in the President's office, a rival State Department has taken shape in recent years. The last three Presidents—but especially Kennedy and Nixon—have relied most heavily upon the White House foreign affairs staff (of considerable size) rather than on the labyrinthian State Department. This curious superimposition of another structure to perform the major planning, analysis, and advice-giving functions of the "official" State Department is the ultimate vote of no confidence. If emulation is the sincerest form of flattery, duplication of effort is the clearest form of institutionalized doubt.

It is paradoxical that the State Department should be singled out as the department having perhaps the most established and traditional ways of doing things in all fields, including selection of personnel. The argument for innovation and pluralism is exceptionally strong here. The ultimate test of effectiveness is in policy output terms in an era in which popular opinion plays a broad and growing role in most countries. This elemental fact should lead to different and more broadly conceived ways of approaching foreign policy. The symbolization and personification of American society is a primary role of any diplomat. The Rogers Act (1924) expressly recognized this, even in a less public relations-conscious era, by requiring geographic representativeness.

[25] James L. McCamy, *Conduct of the New Diplomacy* (New York: Harper & Row, 1964), Chaps. 14 and 15.

In spite of this, the Foreign Service has tended to emphasize broad generalist knowledge, extensive foreign travel, and knowledge of languages—all valuable but in fact not invaluable assets. It has been reluctant to admit offsetting advantages. More than that, it has been characterized—and there is evidence to support this no doubt overgeneralized claim—as being concerned with recruitment of a type based on a mythological American image of a standard personality of inevitably conformist features. That is to say, while the official policy set up a standard diversity, the operating standard was a cultural, ethnic, and class uniformity. The irony is that one of the jobs of these standard men was to propagate the pluralistic ethos of American society. In this respect, the personnel chosen are rather more eloquent than words—"what you are speaks so loudly I cannot hear what you are saying." A black diplomat in Scandinavia can speak only English and still deal with the issue of racism with more impact than a white who speaks the local language—all other things being equal.

This curious myopia and willingness to accept its own articulated norms is not limited, however, to the U.S. State Department. Throughout the world departments of foreign affairs exhibit great inertia and strong class bias. Their awesome responsibilities and great need for qualified talent and experience make them peculiarly resistant to popular pressures and populistic designs. Their roles and functions produce and encourage social protocol and modes of operation that easily degenerate into social, intellectual, and cultural snobbism. Unfortunately this also breeds policy error, paralysis or distortion of information channels, and a strong class bias in the interpretation of events and implementation of policies. In these aspects, universal bureaucratic and organizational tendencies have prevailed over articulated policies and conscious administrative efforts (for instance, those of Averill Harriman in the Kennedy years). This situation had had unfortunate consequences for the United States and it would appear for the State Department as well.

Low-status agencies on the other hand are peculiarly susceptible to pressures, both political and economic. Both the Veterans' Administration and the General Services Administration drastically altered their attitudes and personnel practices as their jobs began to become economically less attractive. The Department of Agriculture, the Navy, and the Federal Trade Commission have also responded to lowered political power and criticism of their general policies by making more sensitive responses to pressures and by instituting more equitable employment practices. On the other hand, prestigious operations like the Air Force, the Department of Justice generally, but especially the FBI, and the Civil Service Commission itself have been slow to respond to pressures to reflect diverse social groups.

## VI.   THE GOALS AND MECHANISMS
## OF REPRESENTATIVENESS

Since World War II, the professed egalitarian aims of the American bureaucracy have been steadily intensified and made more precise.[26] The mechanisms chosen to effectuate these changes have been less well agreed upon, and considerable backing and filling has been the order of the day. Multiple and conflicting agencies have not been uncommon.

The positive injunction to employ solely on grounds of merit is as old as the Pendleton Act. Specific injunctions about specific discriminations were added a half-century later. These reflected the sad truth that the social customs of segregation and discrimination prevailed over the nominal standard of merit. When these failed to produce significant results, special machinery was established separate from the employing agencies to hear complaints. Clearly, in the initial phases it was illogical to expect such agencies as the Civil Service Commission, which had helped create and perpetuate the original pattern of discriminatory employment, to be able to treat complaints in a judicious and objective manner. Complainants could not have confidence in such a system nor could they feel a sense of equity when they were forced to plead a case before those by whom they felt wronged. A Congress paralyzed by Southern seniority and the threats of filibusters failed to act for two decades after World War II, so special presidentially appointed committees to monitor and investigate complaints were the order of the day.

Under Eisenhower, Kennedy, and Johnson the complaints were mainly opening wedges to deal with generalized practices rather than with real remedies for the complainants. As time went on the realization set in that a case-by-case approach was a slow, limited method of dealing with a broad social problem. The emphasis under Kennedy and Johnson shifted to "affirmative action," in which positive recruitment, particularly at medium and high levels, was sought for Blacks. This was accompanied by even more strenuous efforts to separate and distinguish equal employment officers with these unique functions from normal employment and personnel officers; to help evaluate performance, a census of minority employment was instituted. As these tactics bore limited fruit, the President's Committee on Equal Employment Opportunity expanded the scope of its interest to deal with Chicanos, Orientals, and other minorities. A separate structure was created to deal with women in the federal service. At the same time the Civil Rights Commission continued to maintain its authority to study and criticize specific agencies and the program in general.

[26] David H. Rosenbloom, *Federal Service and the Constitution* (Ithaca, N.Y.: Cornell University Press, 1971).

The existence of the dual employment structures was a source of controversy and political pressure. Personnel officers felt, not without reason, that the existence of the rival equal employment officers constituted a vote of no confidence in their own lack of prejudice. In essence, they argued that the past record of prejudice by personnel officers had reflected the real policy preferences of their superiors, not the personnel officers' personal idiosyncrasies. Now that real policy—not merely paper declarations—had changed they were prepared to effectuate it vigorously. The lingering distrust of the black community seemed to them misplaced. These antagonisms on the part of those primarily involved in the employment process and in the minority communities created something less than ideal circumstances.

At the same time outright opponents of civil rights were able to hide behind diversionary slogans, notably the cries of lack of efficiency and reverse discrimination. High-placed Southern congressional leaders, especially committee chairmen, were able to raise specific instances of irregularity, perhaps with the aid of dissidents within the bureaucracy.

The bottleneck of seniority and the filibuster had meant the separate structure was created and financed by presidential order; its personnel were borrowed from elsewhere and this too was a source of grievance and an Achilles heel to the whole operation. The actual sums expended by the Committee were considerable but were buried in the appropriations of eighteen different departments. Senator Willis Robertson (Democrat of Virginia), nominally in protest against presidential misuse of funds, in Spring, 1964, moved to cut each agency's appropriation by the amount contributed to the Committee. Vice-President Humphrey, chairman of the President's Committee, obtained a three-month moratorium on this death sentence. After a study of the situation, Humphrey recommended to President Johnson that the Committee be abolished, with the contract compliance division moved into the Department of Labor and the federal employment function restored to the Civil Service Commission.[27]

The transfer of the function to the Commission was seen as a personal defeat for the Vice-President and the civil rights effort generally. It marked the end of the clearly differentiated structure. And though the Commission made grave and aggressive noises at the beginning, its performance has been lackluster. It has twice failed to meet its own goals for minority employment in its own staff, hardly an inspiring example. Also, after announcing with some fanfare a system of awards for executive achievement in the field of minority employment, awards were not made in successive years, without explanation.[28]

[27] For further details see my *The Negro in Federal Employment* (Minneapolis: University of Minnesota Press, 1967), pp. 39–45.

[28] Robert Vaughn, *The Spoiled Service* (Washington, D.C.: Public Interest Research Group, mimeo, 1972, III), p. 26.

All of this is in a sense irrelevant. The momentum of change now seems sufficient to require little new in the way of propellants. While the federal service has grown only slightly, and even declined in some years, minority employment has grown. Even a pronounced shift in the composition of the service, with the elimination of a large number of unskilled and semiskilled positions, has not prevented the increase in minority employment. Though minority employees were disproportionately found in the ranks of the eliminated positions, gains elsewhere have more than offset those losses. Indeed, this has helped change the pattern of such employment even more rapidly. The newly found managerial-level positions constitute an ever-larger proportion of all minority posts. And recruitment into the middle-range, promotable, semitrainee ranks means that future improvement can confidently be predicted at the upper managerial levels as well.

The Nixon years have been a period of striking gains by the Chicano or Spanish-speaking community. In part, this reflects the lateness of the effort and the large number of people that could be involved for the first time. It is, for example, more difficult to increase absolute numbers of Blacks because of their relative overrepresentation in the service, and rather easier to improve their scantier representation at the upper levels. The administration has been especially aggressive in seeking out and expanding Chicano employment during the years of shrinking federal employment. It has been quite conscious of the political advantages to be gained just as the Johnson administration took full advantage of its achievement among blacks.

While the Civil Service Commission could look reasonably successful statistically by just letting past effort have its delayed effects, it has not escaped criticism nor been immune from competitors. The Equal Employment Opportunities (EEO) Commission was created by the Civil Rights Act of 1964; it was the first break in the dam of Southern dominance of Congress. The functions it absorbed include those which passed from the President's Committee on Contract Compliance to the President's Committee on Equal Employment to the Department of Labor. The broad sweep of its authority could easily be interpreted to include government employment. The presence of the EEO Commission offstage is well known to the Civil Service Commission.

Indeed, it was to avoid loss of the program to the EEO Commission that the Civil Service Commission accepted the concept of establishing goals for minority and women employees—a step which opponents deride as quotas.[29] In essence, we have something like the Philadelphia Plan, but for government instead of private employment. An assessment is made of available man-

[29] David H. Rosenbloom "The Civil Service Commission's Decision to Authorize the Use of Goals and Timetables in the Federal Equal Opportunity Program," unpublished manuscript, 1972.

power, past inequities are assessed, and future goals are established by the agency involved. The Civil Service sets a wide zone of reasonable compliance. The goals are targets and failure to achieve them is acceptable if a good-faith effort is made. Indeed, the Commission has failed to meet several of its own targets.

The progression from elimination of prejudice as a criterion toward an attitude of favorable bias is viewed with mixed feelings on all sides. It has come in gradual steps, each an unfolding of previous positions without close consideration of implications. All sides have been guilty of ill-considered rhetoric. At one time the position currently espoused by the Commission was labeled "compensatory." It was attacked as an improper standard with no limit, an ominous cry for untold and untollable reparations for generations of inequity.[30] Today the position is more properly seen as remedial. That is, most-favored treatment is seen as necessitated by past discrimination. Just as the courts have forbidden actions otherwise acceptable—testing using paper and pencil exams—in a context of previous discrimination, so we may take positive steps to eliminate the accrued disadvantages. The quotalike aspect is relevant only because of past discrimination. Once equality is reached presumably the program should disappear. (Because Blacks are, as we have noted, disproportionately represented in federal service, the logic of the pure quota position would be that efforts should still be made to elevate their status but their recruitment should be discouraged.)

## VII.  CONCLUSIONS

Kingsley's view of the American bureaucracy as the model of representativeness for a civil service undoubtedly had considerable merit but was not without its ironies. Clearly the bureaucracy was both class-, ethnic-, and sex-biased at the time he wrote.

In the light of tighter, more exacting standards, the American political system has moved to dilute the grossest forms of that bias. The effort has been both to increase total participation by various groups and to augment their numbers in higher decision-making echelons. At least statistically, the program has been largely successful; qualitatively the going is almost certainly rougher and less certain, but undoubtedly progress is there.

At the same time, continuous tampering with the principal of merit has its danger too. Institutionalization of representation-by-quota as, for example, in the McGovern-Fraser guidelines for the Democratic Party, has philosophic overtones and structural costs in terms of efficiency. (These are different for a political party than for an operating permanent organization,

[30] Krislov, *The Negro in Federal Employment*, pp. 75–85.

of course.) An open society is likely to be one in which rough representativeness is achieved through offsetting inequalities, rather than through assignment of functions on a structured, almost lotterylike-basis. Allocation of position by social group seems more appropriate to legislative and other political units rather than to the presumably efficient agencies. Nor are such special categories easily created. They can easily involve psychic costs to both those given preference and those disadvantaged. Since the social and political power of the two groups is in disjunction to the policy, its success depends upon an acceptance and tolerance that is decidedly uncommon.

Oddly these new thrusts are most applauded by those who wish to eliminate most of the social basis for political allocation. They recognize just a few distinctions and these they elevate into encrusted near-absolutes. Somehow old age has not been truly brought into the orbit of protected classifications. The classificatory homogenization of various East European and other nonmainstream ethnics under the rubric of "caucasian" hides disproportions of the highest magnitude. Nor have Indians benefited from a serious effort to secure representation. Of course, carried to its logical extreme, the game of quotas would lead us back to an ascriptive society, a truly Levantine social structure where birth and background are the determinants of position.

Oddly too, we must note that Kingsley saw representativeness as a guarantee of responsiveness and obedience to political tides and outcomes. His fear was that insular and isolated bureaucrats would follow their own aims, not those of the body politic. Today's most puristic espousers of representativeness—for example, Nader's Raiders—demand insulation of these bureaucrats, so they can pursue their own view of the public good.[31] As Kingsley saw better than they, the strength of our system has come with adherence to majority policy-making. The diagnosis that the federal system is too permeable and responsive is seldom uniformly applied by critics—all too often they also rely on the opposite assertion. This is hardly impressive to most close observers of our political regime who know how often callousness is present. The attempt to secure a representational but nonresponsive bureaucracy is a perversion of goals, and a self-contradictory approach. Rather, it would appear we should insist on a more balanced cry: above all else, responsiveness—but responsiveness through increased representativeness.

[31] See Theodore J. Lowi, *The End of Liberalism* (New York: W. W. Norton, 1969) for the most profound of such arguments.

# Conclusions

## I. THEORETICAL OVERVIEW

In his magisterial essay "Political Orientations of Bureaucracies in Centralized Empires," Samuel Eisenstadt has suggested bureaucracies may be analyzed in terms of their orientation:

> (a) maintenance of service orientations to both the rulers and the major strata (with, in the societies studied here, usually greater emphasis on services to the rulers); (b) development into a merely passive tool of the ruler with but little internal autonomy or performance of services to the different strata of the population; (c) displacement of bureaucracies' service goals to various strata and to the rulers in favor of goals of self-aggrandizement and usurpation of power exclusively in its own favor and/or in favor of a group with which it becomes closely identified; (d) displacement of bureaucracies' service goals to the major strata in favor of goals of self-aggrandizement and attainment of political power—but together with maintenance of service goals to the rulers.[1]

[1] Samuel Eisenstadt, *Essays on Comparative Institutions* (New York: John Wiley, 1965), p. 220.

If we were Aristotelians, or even Platonists, we could refine these categories into "good" and "bad" regimes, or at any rate into forms of orientation and allegiance that would contain strong possibilities for societal disequilibrium or impediments to progress. Orientation toward a ruler or regime may involve service and dedication on the one hand or servility on the other. Similarly, bureaucratic involvement may take the form of orientation toward professionalism or crass class selfishness.

The thesis advanced here is that those disequilibria, or "bad" tendencies, are associated with nonrepresentativeness, and that *ceteris paribus* representativeness minimizes those distortions. In this sense it is a clearly Aristotelian (and even Madisonian) analysis now applied to bureaucracies.

We have noted certain functional and political limits to the notion of bureaucracy. These are in part alterable as societal changes occur and in part seemingly inherent, at least so far as we know. It is within these realistic limits that these perhaps idealistic ends can be sought.

The methods by which representativeness can be sought are, of course, as varied as the societal and historical settings with which one is concerned. Fundamental to the question are the modes of recruitment. As we have seen, recruitment can be made a method of expansion or constriction of representation virtually at will. Ascription—that is, limiting choice to socially or extraneously defined characteristics rather than those functional to the position—can be utilized as a regime prefers. In a caste system where, say, a Brahmin or a Mandarin alone may qualify, it is of course contractive of the range of representation. A quota system on the other hand may enhance representativeness as well as restrict it. American society has generally rejected quotas as a desirable policy, perhaps because it is a snake pit full of dangerous creatures, but other societies have found such arrangements feasible and at least in the short run highly functional. More (or less) representative recruitment may involve expansion in size, simple replacement over time, or enforced replacement at a pace determined by the regime. Total or extremely large-scale turnover is of course a rather good index of a social revolution. Another course might be adoption of a new policy or intensification of an old one as in, for example, the 1952 creation of the Department of Health, Education and Welfare with the parallel growth in federal governmental involvement in support of education.

In general, recruitment seems close to a necessary (though it is clearly not a sufficient) condition for representativeness. "Virtual representation," by which the decision-makers emphatically project views of others, or semi-official cooptative consulting devices, do not seem to be effective over any prolonged period (for example, over a generation), and they decay with a rapid half-life.

Admission into standard decision units may be enhanced or diminished by shifts in the pattern of units involved in key decisions or the processes by which decisions are made. We may witness a form of this reality if the emerging black majorities in core urban areas succeed in electing black mayors, but political and economic realities diminish the importance and latitude of big-city mayors. On the other hand, a process of consulting for views may become a form of veto, thus expanding the power of the consulted party with only a very subtle change in decision processes. But real shifts in power will ultimately be reflected in institutional patterns.

The insistence on participation has two aspects. The first is the simple affirmation that all groups have a right, an access, to position and influence. For this aspect—symbolic and legitimizing—I have suggested the term "representational" participation. But as David Truman has pointed out, access to decision-making is a good index to ultimate influence and is valued in its own right.[2] The second type therefore is the active, "functional," robust participation of groups in concrete decisions. This can occur through consultative mechanisms, of course, but it is surer and steadier when the desired diversity is a living reality. The argument for *representational* participation, in short, is that it leads to *functional* effectiveness. Fredrick Mosher makes much the same point by referring to "passive" or sociological representation and "active" representation, where an interest is vigorously pursued.[3]

While some forms of interest representation have had paralyzing, polarizing, and dysfunctional effects, the basic activity seems essential to the operation of any society. Those who have attempted to analyze society in terms of group activity and group pressure have found the tool as sharp (and as dull) in less developed as well as more developed societies.

Finally we must note the "ratchet effect" involved in governmental recognition or withdrawal of power for a group. There is a significant social "multiplier effect" in what is politically done both because such actions tend to be highly visible and because they tend to be enveloped in the invisible rays of legitimacy. What government does is what fixes social policy. The treatment of its constituent individuals and constituent groups in political form is a tip-off and a harbinger of social action in other guises.

It is a "chicken or the egg" question as to whether in this process government precedes or creates smaller social units, or whether the smaller groups are in some genuine sense building blocks of the larger society. In either event, it is clear that the touchstone of power and legitimacy is recognition by the agency that is involved in rationing "the authoritative allocation of values." A group with power will be recognized governmentally and vice versa. There will be a tendency for actual power and its visibility to seek a common level.

[2] David Truman, *The Governmental Process* (New York: Knopf, 1952).
[3] Fredrick Mosher, *Democracy and the Public Service* (New York: Oxford University Press, 1968), pp. 11–14.

With respect to public bureaucracies, societies have immense powers to effect change with spillover into the broader society. The English gentry decided to expand social participation to encompass a newly emergent urban-based middle class. They restructured not only the civil service but also its ancillary training schools, and even the broad field of public and private education. Girding for battle in contrast, the Junker and Japanese elites entrenched themselves in such structures. The results of such policies are clearly seen throughout the history of these countries. Options are thus easily available to decision-makers—within the highly latitudinarian bounds of functional necessity—to construct a purist, a self-serving, or a deliberately, even neurotically, responsive bureaucratic structure. Tables of organization are not fashioned in heaven; neither are their dimensions immutable.

## II. THE JUSTIFICATION OF BUREAUCRATIC INCLUSIVENESS

At first glance "representative bureaucracy" appears to be an oxymoron, inherently contradictory like "cold heat" or, *pace* Mr. Chief Justice Warren, "deliberate speed." Bureaucracies handle matters, perform functions, and are meant to do and be, not represent or mean or symbolize. The functional necessities of such structures presumably dominate their human aspects. The "political" branches seem the places for such participatory relationships.

But our second look has indicated that societal tensions, rates of participation, and exclusions are, in fact, part and parcel of bureaucratic relationships. Furthermore, we have touched on the evidence indicating that bureaucratic effectiveness at the societal level—the degree of governmental penetration in societal interaction—is also related to participation in the bureaucracy. Homogenized bureaucracies run the risk of getting better and better at performing tasks which other people regard as of increasingly less importance. When new winds sweep through such structures, they not only infuse fresh thoughts. By their momentum they also have the potential of spreading the effectiveness and purpose of the structure, so that its external reach is extended. In such a process, representativeness is a two-way conduit.

The bureaucracy then emerges as a good, even superior, index of societal cohesion and diffusion. It looms as a more stable and reliable measure of social power than elite studies of legislative bodies or of small inner-circle groups typically examined; further, the requirements for participation turn out to be less rather than more restrictive than legislative or strictly executive roles. Youth, left-handers, atomic physicists, and even classicists are more commonly found in the dusty halls of executive office buildings than in the debating halls of lawmakers. Since bureaucracies are both more stable and better defined than other forms of broad participation, they constitute a more practical index than even voter turnout or more nebulous—though probably more significant—forms of political behavior.

We have also touched upon—but for reasons of economy and logical development have not fully developed—the argument that social participation in the service is a reasonable approximation in mirror-image of the impact of bureaucracy upon society. In politics as in life one casts one's bread upon the waters with reasonable but unsure expectation that the return will be related to investment although sometimes we fail· and get back that clear alternative: soggy bread. A successful system transmutes access into satisfaction; a successful repressive system transmutes nonparticipation into passive acceptance.

## III. SOME RESEARCH POSSIBILITIES

The degree of active participation numerically and in terms of level permits the development of an index of political participation, which in turn—hypothetically at least—measures the approximate dispersion of policy through society. Development of a similar satisfaction index leads to the possibility of then measuring something approximating quality of policy decisions and effectiveness.

One of the most intriguing unused concepts, developed particularly for studies of colonial systems, is the notion of the "dual polity" in parallel to the notion of the "dual economy." These concepts may well have been disguised apologia for Dutch colonial separatism and maintenance of power. From a nonideological standpoint, though, it suggests a generalized problem: the degree to which access to power is open or closed in a society. In such an anlysis "pluralism" may be asserted with equal plausibility. In any event, the bureaucracy, with relatively open stratification and identifiable occupants, would seem to afford an opportunity for comparatively precise characterization of social systems.

The potential here is reinforced by the development of measures to deal with precisely these sorts of problems in Douglas Rae and Michael Taylor's *The Analysis of Political Cleavages.*[4] Their principal measure is that of "fragmentation," $F$, which is defined as "the preparation of all pairs . . . which join members from different groups" or, more formally,

$$F = \frac{\text{number of mixed pairs}}{\text{total number of pairs}}$$

[4] Douglas Rae and Michael Taylor, *The Analysis of Political Cleavages* (New Haven, Conn.: Yale University Press, 1972).

In a group of 10 individuals where the cleavage analyzed is skin color and there are 4 blacks, 4 whites, and 2 orientals, the number of racially matched pairs is 13 and of mixed types (e.g., black and white, oriental and black, etc.,), 32; F = .71.

This simple measure permits the development of an overall index of both societal and bureaucratic fractionalization. The two indices can then be compared with respect to their congruity and a host of possible relationships are at least theoretically testable. While the available data fall far short of leading to strong and accurate statements, they are improving. Future research is not only feasible, but is imperative—and actually underway.[5]


## IV.  SOME POLICY IMPLICATIONS—ESPECIALLY FOR THE UNITED STATES

Many societies—not just the United States—are currently adjusting their policies and their thinking because of emerging social groups, and because of the equality revolution which is part of modern society. To some the only reality is accomplishments and percentages, with all else verbiage and semantics. The view developed here is that what we do is highly significant but how we think about it is probably even more important.

What can be at conflict is the notion of individual versus group achievement; we may witness in short a reversal of the nineteenth-century English jurist and historian Sir Henry Maine's notion that civilization is a transition "from status to contract." In many areas, for example, regulation of insurance companies and the recognition of labor unions, Maine's formulation of what is "modern" seems sloganizing and even a bit fatuous. But on the basic worth of the individual and as a plea for self-realization it looms as even more necessary today. The threat from notions of quotas and proper allocations is well expressed by Milton Himmelfarb: "Equality and justice used to mean No Discrimination (against individuals), now they tend to mean Fair Shares (for groups). How does one assure Fair Shares? By legislating proportionality, or quotas." [6] "Fair Shares" is, in fact, a substitution of a new perspective, not merely an additional criterion. It asserts the primacy of the social interrelationships radiating outward over the immediate and more tangible job nexus. As indicated throughout this book, that view is quite rational—contrary to the views of some of its critics. Indeed, in many ways the notion of quotas must be resisted in part because it is too rational. To consider all the ramifications of all public officeholding and to hold that

---

[5] See, for example, the promising beginnings in Alvin Rabushka and Kenneth Shepsle, *Politics in Plural Societies: Theory of Democratic Instability* (Columbus, Ohio: Charles E. Merrill, 1972).

[6] Milton Himmelfarb, "McGovern and the Jews," *Commentary*, Vol. 54, September 1972, 48–52.

anything that has social consequences may be taken into account threatens individuality, professionalism, and objective standards. Even if such widespread considerations are limited to those cases where, as in race, there is a recognizable public policy, there are serious consequences that flow from the disruption of a somewhat artificially conceived system of relatively well defined and delimited standards.

## V.  WHO IMPOSES WHAT QUOTAS?—A VITAL QUESTION

1. The world experience with quota systems is decidedly mixed. In both Czarist Russia, where it was overt policy, and in Soviet Russia, where it is covert, it has produced severe disaffection. Its aim, there as in Malaya, was to protect *politically dominant* groups against effective individual competition from members of less powerful social groupings. In a sense, these quotas emerge as milder forms of South Africa's apartheid or Ugandan expulsion of Asiatics, which are forms of securing monopoly or limited competition from more talented or trained (or, as in South Africa, more trainable) social groups. The disadvantaged understand what is being done to them. The acceptance of superior political power is quite as would be expected—cynical, rueful, and not just a bit contemptuous.

2. Quotas may also be imposed as a direct result of bargaining and accommodation among groups sharing power. Here its acceptance tends to be more positive, even if exact allocation may be less than perfect. The example par excellence is Lebanon. Without such accommodation it is hard to see how that society could have survived. Israel, Belgium, and Canada are now in various forms moving into such accommodations with majority populations, whose political power has been less than their numerical proportion.

The desirability of political sharing is clear. The danger (as reflected by Lebanon) of static arrangements—which all too easily become outmoded—is also clear. The more explicit the bargain struck, the harder it is to adjust to new realities. The lines of the agreement, the fault lines along which cleavages are recognized, are thereby intensified and made deeper and broader. Ambiguity of arrangements with genuine sharing has been the most successful mode where it has worked. While it is viewed with suspicion, it can be the bridge by which essential fusion of the society is accomplished. But that ambiguity may be politically tolerable and workable only in a society not already too badly divided, where trust is not eroded. A mild medicine may cure more often than a strong one precisely because it is prescribed for less severe illnesses.

3. The third situation combines elements of bargaining and—depending upon one's point of view—enlightened self-interest or paternalism. A *minority*

*group* seeks and obtains some greater share of the political and fiscal resources available in the society. India and the United States are the principal exemplars of this situation. In one sense the quest for opportunity that is not racially bound is, as Harry Kalven has beautifully put it, "an attempt to entrap democracy in its own decencies." In a future-oriented sense it is an anticipation of avoidance of social disturbance and continuous discord. In India the problem of the untouchables both quantitatively and qualitatively has been and remains greater than that of the nonwhites in the United States. The possible exception to this generalization is in the relative expectations of the have-nots, particularly the time frame in which expectations have been cast. By and large, American promises and dreams of the sixties seem to have been more extravagantly phrased and more decisively dashed.

In India quotas have clearly caused problems, but the period of their implementation has also witnessed progress. The relentless pursuit of advantage for the disadvantaged has been carried down into the level of schools and into the electoral system just as well as it has been pursued with respect to the bureaucracy. A deterioration of effectiveness both in the schools and the Civil Service has been evident. This is at least in part a degeneration caused by removal of British standards (without an internal substitute) and is in no clear way a product of compensatory preference. At the same time the formal requirements for registration and certification both of "backward peoples" and of individuals as members of such groups cause considerable psychic tension. The "benefited" feel they must betray themselves, and label themselves for all to see as inferior. And those of the "privileged" class who must yield special advantages find their situation perverse and unreal. After a slow start the untouchables have begun to reap some advantage in a situation which was depressed and in which initial progress was most difficult. The hardening of community lines, a movement toward dualism, is apparent however even in the change in the electoral system.

Under the guise of "goals" the United States has also moved toward something of a quota system. While "goals" have been distinguished in terms of not setting maxima for any group or requiring strict adherence in any time frame, the fact is that India has also operated with those qualifications and forthrightly called such "guidelines" quotas. Yet there are other qualifications that are also consequential. In most instances the base for measuring "fair shares" is determined by the portion of the available qualified work force made up by the group involved. It is their share of those who have met minimal qualifications, rather than the share of the general population, that is calculated for the "Philadelphia Plan" and such derivatives as the Department of Health, Education and Welfare's guidelines for universities and colleges. There are inferences generally derived from such data that a group not holding its fair share is being discriminated against either through direct unfairness or through the operations of a nebulous entity, "the system," in one of its synonyms. Such inferences are not, strictly speaking, justifiable, though the more closely two populations are matched in terms of objective criteria, the more valid the inference becomes. Clearly, the pool of available qualified workers presents a better base for judging fairness than the general public, though it still is far from a matched set of populations. The inference may then perhaps be softened to suggest that less effort in recruitment than what was sought as a matter of good social policy has been expended.

Again, the "guidelines" notion has been instituted with a sense that the action is both remedial—after finding fault in either the strong or weak senses cited above—and temporary. Once some sort of rough justice is achieved for minorities and women in most areas, presumably the apparatus would be dismantled. The Indian experience here has been somewhat disheartening; though the constitution of India provided a time limit for special privilege, that time was later expanded as has been the domain of privilege. Whether that experience is apropos depends in part on whether one views the Indian problem as a deeper and less corrigible one.

If the coming of such standards is permanent and is viewed as a substitute for competence, then the worst fears of their critics will be realized. The question is whether "fair shares" is reconcilable with individual achievement and the requisite efficiency of governmental and other structures, or whether it is a rival, overriding, and preeminent standard. In a sense quotas—and the use of euphemisms may be significant here—can be regarded as a temporary means to assure equal opportunity, or as an end in themselves. The danger of the first departure is that "temporary" attitudes, like temporary buildings and emergency taxes, all too often remain as long or longer than permanent ones.

The argument for "fair shares" numerically expressed is a pragmatic and powerful one. If competence were easily measured, and if the surrogates of education and experience were both tightly related to performance and equitably distributed, and if recruitment were a simple objective process, the case would be much weaker. In fact none of these are true. Paper-and-pencil or other tests are positively but weakly related to performance. So are previous experience and education and training. And whatever the formal process of recruitment, the informal arrangements are often more significant in determining who actually gets the job. For example, the grapevine can tip off a friend to appear at the right moment. To compensate for a predominantly white network of informal recruitment we might, for example, intensify the formal processes in the black community.

Thus it is not merely a question of "competence" versus "social justice." It is a complex question as to whether the normal "objective" way of evaluation can be accommodated to more accurately strain out justice. When that process is indicted and is on the defensive, then other considerations may loom as legitimate and even preeminent in face of lack of confidence in the very nature of the selection criteria. The past few years have seen such a crisis of confidence in the Civil Service Commission itself over its methods, and only recently has it felt that it had by careful combination of various modes of testing come up with a defensible package of appropriate selection processes. But even defensible accuracy is far short of complete accuracy. And as we have argued earlier, "performance" is not just the carrying out of narrowly defined tasks.

The persistence of ambiguity in all these aspects creates both a need and a justification for "fair shares." Because it is so easy to simulate good faith in recruitment efforts and recruitment of the best, it is also easy to suspect that neither criterion has been met. So results are virtually the only final measure of good faith. Similarly, because failure to choose the truly best qualified is inevitable, a little more use of extraneous criteria seems more justifiable.

The argument against quotas is even clearer. Such hardening of the categories is the arteriosclerosis of society, belying concepts of merit and achievement. Furthermore it tends to convert the issue of just treatment from a visible individual matter to an abstract, nebulous, and completely politicized one, where ingenuity in argument will be more significant than assiduousness in performance. Such a situation is probably not politically sustainable for long even when, as in Israel, for example, it is the majority that is socially disadvantaged, and *a fortiori* where, as in the United States, it is a small minority. Nor is the continuous heaping and recapitulating of grievances, the vying for still greater proofs of backwardness and deprivation, conducive to a proud, free, and vibrant society. Whether institutionalizing a disease is a method of cure is doubtful. To the degree that particularistic criteria—race, sex, and the like—are recognized they may become encrusted, encouraging rather than discouraging discrimination and disharmony.

Caught between policies which serve to lull a complacent majority or which could corrupt the human relations of majority and minority, our system has elected a middle course, practically and semantically. Thus the concept of goals is extended to most but not all positions of public responsibility; the base of expectations has been the pool of qualified persons rather than the general population; and the achievement of a specific numeric level at a specified time is not rigorously enforced. The avoidance of the language of quotas is itself significant.

Evidence would suggest, though hardly prove, that this is basically a sound orientation. The ultimate test will be to translate this into an effective time frame. We need policies that permit the necessary social accommodation of groups formerly excluded into a fair share of the decision-making positions and functions within a reasonable period of time, without basic distortion of the principles of merit and justice. Because numbers are the easy game, we have made greater statistical than real progress. Qualitative improvement in the types of positions is even more needed than the doling out of second-rate positions. Because individual justice and merit are not always determinable, we have finessed the question of the ultimate effects on basic values of temporary practices—practices which might easily become institutionalized. In this respect there is a reconciliation of goals. For the minority it is vital to achieve substantial parity as rapidly as possible. It is also in the interests of the majority to achieve this through structures and arrangements avowedly remedial, temporary, and disposable.

In this, as in other achievements of status in our society, governmental structures take the leadership. In that sense, too, they function as a representative bureaucracy, the litmus test of our society in success or failure. The task will be—without impairing functional effectiveness and by providing model demonstrations of justifiable and equitable treatment of individuals for our bureaucracy, which is already a leader in its inclusiveness—to become in a fuller sense an even more representative bureaucracy.

# Bibliographics

This volume's basic indebtedness to J. Donald Kingsley's *Representative Bureaucracy* (Yellow Springs, Ohio: Antioch Press, 1944) is rather clear to any reader. Kingsley's work is also good and instructive reading. V. Subramanian's "Representative Bureaucracy: A Reassessment," (*American Political Science Review*, LXI, December 1967, pp. 1010–19) is a helpful updating.

The social background of decision-makers is a favorite topic of social scientists and historians. A highly useful little paperback—though badly in need of updating—is Donald Matthews's *The Social Background of Decision-Makers* (New York: Doubleday, 1954). It summarizes major theoretical approaches and many empirical studies as well. Dwaine Marvick (ed.), *Political Decision-Makers* (New York: Free Press, 1961) has a number of discrete studies. T. R. Bottomore's *Elites and Society* (New York: Basic Books, 1964) is a brilliant, taut, and penetrating discussion of the entire area of privilege and power. Suzanne Keller's *Beyond the Ruling Class* (New York: Random House, 1963) is a more discursive study of elite theory. The above books provide leads into the works of Pareto, Mosca, and Michels but should be supplemented by James Burnham's *The Machiavellians* (New York: John Day Company, 1943) and his *Managerial Revolution* (New York: John Day Company, 1941) as both primary and secondary sources.

There are countless studies of specific bureaucracies. Johanna Menzel (ed.) *The Chinese Civil Service* (Boston: Heath, 1963) is an absorbing collection of such materials on the ancient, imperial Chinese bureaucracy and is therefore a most interesting example of what can be assembled from existing histories. Some more contemporary, representative studies of more than passing interest include: Morroe Berger, *Bureaucracy and Society in Modern Egypt*, (Princeton, N.J.: Princeton University Press, 1957); Robert Tilman, *Bureaucratic Transition in Malaya*, (Durham, N.C.: Duke University Press, 1964); William Robson (ed.) *The Civil Service in Britain and France*, (London: Hogarth Press, 1956); Roger Kelsall, *Higher Civil Servants in Britain from 1872 to the Present Day*, (London: Routledge & Kegan Paul, 1955); George K. Schueller, *Politburo*, (Stanford, Calif.: Stanford University Press, 1951); and John A. Porter, *The Vertical Mosaic*, (Toronto: University of Toronto Press, 1965).

Ralph Braibanti's collection, *Asian Bureaucratic Systems Emergent from the British Imperial Tradition*, (Durham, N.C.: Duke University Press, 1966) deals with transitional bureaucracies. Brian Chapman's *The Profession of Government* (London: Allen & Unwin, 1963) is unexcelled in its general coverage of this point, particularly on Western European bureaucracies. This listing hardly begins to cover the many excellent studies of this type, however, since this is one of the rare topics in social science that is both well studied and studied well. In a sense it is an elevated form of social gossip, which attracts attention from writer and reader alike.

The American bureaucracy has had the lion's share of such studies. The most comprehensive are Franklin Kilpatrick, *et al.*, *The Image of the Federal Service*, (Washington, D.C.: Brookings, 1964) and W. Lloyd Warner, *et al.*, *The American Federal Executive* (New Haven, Conn.: Yale University Press, 1963). Also see Reinhard Bendix's *Higher Civil Servants in American Society* (Boulder, Colo.: University of Colorado Press, 1949) and Dean Mann's more limited *The Assistant Secretaries* (Washington, D.C.: Brookings, 1965).

More general works are also useful. Paul Van Riper's *History of the United States Civil Service* (Evanston: Row, Peterson & Co., 1958) is the most comprehensive on the American bureaucracy, and Leonard White's fine series, including *The Federalists* and *The Jeffersonians*, (New York: Macmillan, 1948 and 1951, respectively) is the most broadly conceived of historical treatment. Fredrick Mosher's *Democracy and the Public Service* (New York: Oxford University Press, 1968) is a thoughtful introduction to many value questions including some covered in this volume.

For some comprehensive approaches to bureaucracies see Robert Merton, *et al.*, *Reader in Bureaucracy* (Glencoe: Free Press, 1952); James March (ed.) *Handbook of Organizations* (Chicago: Rand McNally, 1965); Bertram

Gross, *The Managing of Organizations* (New York: Free Press, 1964); and Peter Blau and W. Richard Scott, *Formal Organizations* (San Francisco: Chandler, 1963), the latter with an outstanding bibliography.

William Niskenan's *Bureaucracy and Representative Government* (Chicago: Aldine-Atherton, 1971) is a distinctive measurement–cost analysis of the problem.

Solomon Fabricant's *The Trend of Governmental Activity in the United States* (New York: National Bureau of Economic Research, 1952) and M. Abromovits and V. Eliasberg's *The Growth of Public Employment in Great Britain* (Princeton, N.J.: Princeton University Press, 1957) constitute pathfinding efforts to trace the extent of operations of government activity.

For historical depth and wide scope Samuel Eisenstadt's *The Political Systems of Empires* (New York: Free Press, 1963) and his *Essays on Comparative Institutions* (New York: John Wiley, 1965) are unexcelled repositories of incredible erudition meshed with useful if sometimes overly subtle taxonomy.

For good treatments of transfer of power and expanding horizons see Reinhard Bendix, *Nation Building and Citizenship* (New York: Doubleday, 1969); T. H. Marshall, *Class, Citizenship and Social Development* (New York, Doubleday, 1964); and S. M. Lipset and R. Bendix, *Social Mobility in Industrial Society* (Berkeley, Calif.: University of California Press, 1959).

Robert Wilkinson's *Gentlemanly Power* (London: Oxford University Press, 1964) is an account of the use of the nineteenth-century British school system as a vehicle of social change. See also Ralph Braibanti (ed.) *Political and Administrative Development* (Durham, N.C.: Duke University Press, 1969) and Joseph LaPalombara (ed.) *Bureaucracy and Political Development* (Princeton, N.J.: Princeton University Press, 1963).

On representation, see Hanna F. Pitkin, *The Concept of Representation* (Berkeley, Calif.: University of California Press, 1967) and A. H. Birch, *Representation and Responsible Government* (Toronto: University of Toronto Press, 1969). The Nomos volume, *Representation*, edited by J. Roland Pennock and John Chapman (New York: Atherton, 1968), has useful, recent contributions on the subject, and Pitkin's edited work *Representation* (New York: Atherton, 1969) contains brief selections from largely classic sources. More modern speculation is contained in Norton Long's *The Polity* (Chicago: Rand McNally, 1962), and Robert G. Dixon's *Democratic Representation* (New York: Oxford University Press, 1968) deals most thoroughly with apportionment and other current disputes.

Krislov's *The Negro in Federal Employment* (Minneapolis: University of Minnesota Press, 1967) and David Rosenbloom's *Federal Service and the Constitution* (Ithaca, N.Y.: Cornell University Press, 1971) both deal with affirmative action.

# Index

141

Carr, E. H., 29
*Caste in India*, 83*fn*
Caste selection processes, Kingsley urges reform of, 12–13
Caste systems, 128
in India, 83–84
Castro, Fidel, 50
*Challenge and Change*, 109, 110*fn*, 113, 115*fn*, 116*fn*, 117*fn*, 118
Chamoun, President of Lebanon, 100
Chapman, Brian, 97, 97*fn*
Chinese, as problem in Malaysia, 88–89
Chomsky, Noam, 9, 9*fn*
*Citizen and the Administrator in a Developing Democracy, The*, 86
*Civic Culture, The*, 65
Civil Rights Commission:
critical role of, 122
problems with, 123
Civil service:
British:
Kingsley's criticism of, 10–11
composition as issue, 8
U.S.:
foundations and growth, 109–10
growing power of, 23
history, 107–10
middle-class professionals in, 54–55
reform as goal of middle class, 108–9
as representative, 104, 105
Civil Service Commission, 123, 136
criticism of, 124
slow response to equitable employment, 121, 122
*Civil Service and the Patronage, The*, 107*fn*, 108*fn*
*Civil Service in the Changing State, The*, 60*fn*, 70*fn*
Clarke, M. J., 26*fn*
Class characteristics, effect of on public service, 54
Classification Act (1923), 114
Clerical help, governmental need for, 47, 48 (*Tab.*)
Closed bureaucracy, in Australia, 49
Coleman, William, 108
Commission on the Status of Women, 114
Committee on Contract Compliance, 124
Committee on Equal Employment Opportunity, 122, 124
Compensatory opportunity, 1, 2
Competence:
criteria, intrinsic and extrinsic, 4–5
perspectives on, 3–4
*Conduct of the New Diplomacy*, 120*fn*
Confessional integration, in Israel, 101–3
Confessionalism, in Lebanon, 97–101

*Congress: The First Branch of Government*, 23*fn*, 52
Congressional committee structure, as modification of popular will, 37–38
Corruption, as factor in Athenian democracy, 45
Cost analysis, as proof of policy desirability, 36
Coxe, Tench, 107
Crow, Ralph E., 98, 99, 99*fn*
Cultural characteristics, effect of on public service, 54
"Cultural pluralism," 18
*Cultural Pluralism and the American Idea*, 19*fn*
Cummings, Milton C. Jr., 48, 115, 115*fn*, 117*fn*, 119, 119*fn*

Davidson, Roger H., 23, 23*fn*, 37, 37*fn*, 52
Davis, Kenneth, 27, 27*fn*
Decision-making:
and larger-unit point of view, 56, 57
and representativeness, 129
Decisions, bureaucratic advantages regarding acceptance, 64
De Gaulle, Charles, 94
De Grazia, Alfred, 23*fn*, 52
Democracy:
bureaucratic power as an issue, 35–36
as form of political agency, 25
*Democracy and the Individual*, 24*fn*
*Democracy and the Public Service*, 129*fn*
Deutsch, Karl, W., 91, 91*fn*
Dickens, Charles, 107, 107*fn*
Discrimination:
agencies against, in U.S., 105
policies against, 58
racial, in U.S., 110–13
Djilas, Milovan, 27, 27*fn*, 28, 29, 29*fn*
"Dual economy," notion of, 131
"Dual polity," notion of, 131
Dushkin, Lelah, 83*fn*, 84, 84*fn*, 85*fn*
Duty variety, as agency characteristic, 33
Duverger, Maurice, 6, 77, 77*fn*

East India Charter Act (1833), 17
East India Company, 17
Education, as equalizer of individual talent, 62
Educational opportunity, effects on administrative class, 11–12
Educational system:
discrimination of in Malaya, 91–92
influence of reforms on representative bureaucracy, 14
Eichner, Alfred S., 19*fn*
Eisenstadt, S. N., 28, 28*fn*, 101*fn*, 127, 127*fn*

Eldersveld, Samuel J., 86
*Election by Lot in Athens*, 43*fn*, 44*fn*
Elections, derided by Long and Mosca,
    39–40
Electoral process, as reflection of popular
    will, 37–38
*Elements of Public Administration*, 69*fn*
Eliasberg, Vera F., 32*fn*, 47*fn*, 51
*Elites and Society*, 29*fn*
Emerson, Rupert, 20, 89, 89*fn*
Employment, modes of entry to, 60
Employment decisions, in federal bureauc-
    racies, 55–58
*Encyclopedia Britannica*, 24, 24*fn*
*End of Liberalism, The*, 126*fn*
Engineer and the Profit System, 29*fn*
England:
    bureaucratic controls in Empire, 17–18
    colonial administration controls:
        India, 17
English, as official language of Canada, 95
Enloe, Cynthia, 92*fn*
Equal Employment Opportunities Com-
    mission, 111, 124, 125
Equality, policy implications, U.S., 132–33
Equal opportunity, 1, 2
Eriksson, Erik M., 108, 108*fn*
*Essays on Comparative Institutions*, 28*fn*, 128*fn*
Ethnic differences, in Israel, 101–3
Eulau, Heinz, 24*fn*
*Executive Civil Service of the United States, The*,
    118
Executive Order 11375, prohibiting dis-
    crimination against women, 114
Executive Order 11478, prohibiting dis-
    crimination against women, 115
Experts (*See also* Technocrats):
    circumscribed role of, 36
    failures of training, 67–68
    governmental need for, 47, 48 (*Tab.*)
*Extraordinary Black Book*, 10

Fabricant, S., 51, 51*fn*, 110*fn*
Fair Employment Commission, 111
"Fair Shares":
    as concept, 132–33
    and individual achievement, 134–36
Fayyad, Halim, 99
F.B.I., slow response to equitable employ-
    ment, 121
Federal employment, projections for future,
    118–19
Federal Equal Employment Opportunity
    program, 115
*Federal Government in Nigeria*, 67*fn*
*Federalists, The*, 107, 107*fn*
*Federal Service and the Constitution*, 122*fn*

*Federal White-Collar Workers*, 117*fn*
*Federal Work Force Outlook*, 118*fn*
Federation, growth of in Belgium, 93
Fish, Carl Russell, 107*fn*, 108*fn*
Fitzgerald, F. Scott, 46
Flemings, and linguistic conflict, 93–94
*Forest Ranger, The*, 75, 75*fn*
Forham, Margery, 67*fn*
"Fragmentation," as measure of societal
    and bureaucratic fractionalization,
    131–32
Freedman, Maurice, 89*fn*
Free Masonry, in France, 97
"Free representation," unique in modern
    times, 25, 26
French-Canadian community, and sepa-
    ratism, 94
French Canadians, represented in bureauc-
    racy, 95–96
Friedrich, Carl, 24, 58*fn*
*From Max Weber*, 26*fn*

GAHAL party, in Israel, 102
Galanter, Marc, 84*fn*
Galbraith, John K., 2, 2*fn*
Gandhi, Mahatma, 83, 84, 87
Gellhorn, Walter, 27*fn*
Generalists, required by bureaucracy, 51
Generalist/specialist relationship, in gov-
    ernment, 67–69
General Services Administration, personnel
    practices, 121
*Gentlemanly Power*, 62*fn*
Gerrymandering, 37
Gerth, H. H., 26*fn*, 30, 30*fn*
Ginzberg, Eli, 19*fn*
Gladstone, William, 11
Governance, support task of, 4–5
Governmental growth, ability to produce
    revenue as determinant, 46–47
*Governmental Process, The*, 129*fn*
*Government and Manpower*, 49*fn*
*Government and Parliament*, 14*fn*
Government bureaucracies, different from
    simpler aggregations, 46
Government of India Act (1935), 83, 84
Governments:
    as monopolies, 51
    vulnerability of, 5
Government service:
    as factor encouraging exclusive member-
        ship, 58–59
    skills needed for, 49
Government structures:
    Communist, 33–34
    developing countries, 34
    Western neocapitalist, 33

"Grade creep," 51
Grant, U. S., 19
Greaves, H. R. G., 60, 60*fn*, 70*fn*
*Greek Commonwealth, The,* 44*fn*
Greening, W. E., 94*fn*
Gross, Bertram, 34, 34*fn*
*Growth of Public Employment in Great Britain, The,* 32*fn*, 47*fn*
Guttsman, W. L., 14*fn*

Hamilton, Alexander, 108
Handicapped, preference for, in legislation, 116–17
Harriman, Averill, 121
Harrison, Evelyn, 110
Haryans, discrimination against, 83, 84
Headlam, James Wycliffe, 43*fn*, 44*fn*
Hegel, Friedrich, 46
Hemingway, Ernest, 46
Hess, Clyde G., 97*fn*, 100*fn*
Hierarchy-command situation, effect on employment practices, 56
Himmelfarb, Milton, 132, 132*fn*
Histadrut, as control in Israel, 101–2
*Historical Statistics of the United States,* 109
*History of the United States Civil Service,* 8*fn*, 109, 111*fn*
Hitler, Adolf, 31, 56, 79
Hoebel, E. Adamson, 53, 53*fn*
Hofstadter, Richard, 108
Hopkins, Harry, 30
Huggett, Frank E., 93*fn*
Humphrey, Hubert, 123
Huntington, Samuel P., 29
Hurewitz, J. C., 98, 98*fn*
Hutton, J. H., 83*fn*
Hyneman, Charles, 35, 35*fn*

Ickes, Harold, 30, 119
Identity of interests, concept of, 23
*Immigrants on the Threshold,* 101*fn*
India:
  minority group quota systems, 134
  provisions on representativeness, 83–88
*India and Ceylon,* 83*fn*, 85*fn*
Indian Nationalist movement, 87
"Indirect rule" concept, in India, 87
*Individual Freedom and Government Restraint,* 27*fn*
*Inequality,* 2*fn*
Inequality, as issue, 2
Inkeles, Alexander, 62, 62*fn*
*Innovation,* 49*fn*
Innovation, and skills required by, 49
*Inside the Third Reich,* 31, 31*fn*
"Institutional racism," in bureaucracies, 71
*Integration and Development in Israel,* 101*fn*

*Interest Groups in Italian Politics,* 79*fn*
Interests, for bureaucratic posts, 53–55
Israel:
  ethnic differences and integration in, 101–3
  quota system, 133, 136
*Israel: Group Relation in a New Society,* 101*fn*

Jackson, Andrew, 108
Jacksonian movement, and public employment, 107–8
James, William, 18, 19*fn*
Jefferson, Thomas, 107, 108
Jeffersonian movement, and public employment, 107–8
Jencks, Christopher, 1, 2*fn*
Jennings, M. Kent, 48, 115*fn*
Jensen-Ferguson Amendment (1951), 8
Job analysis, questioned, 2–3
"Job-skill-related" criteria, 2
Johnson, Lyndon, 111, 114, 115, 122, 123
Jones, A. H. M., 44, 44*fn*, 45, 45*fn*, 83*fn*
Jowett, Benjamin, 17

Kallen, Horace, 18, 19, 19*fn*
Kalven, Harry, 134
Kamin, Leon J., 94, 94*fn*
Kaufman, Herbert, 75, 75*fn*
Kennedy, John F., 120, 122
Kennedy, Robert, 111
Kilpatrick, Franklin P., 48, 106, 115*fn*
King, MacKenzie, 95
Kingsley, J. Donald, 10, 11, 11*fn*, 12, 12*fn*, 13, 13*fn*, 14, 15, 16, 39, 61*fn*, 104, 105, 125, 126
Kosygin, Aleksei, 31
Krislov, Samuel, 2*fn*, 15*fn*, 30*fn*, 125*fn*
Kristol, Irving, 2
Kroef, Justus van der, 92*fn*

Labour party, 10
Language:
  as barrier in government, 73
  effects on Malay unification, 90–91
Lansbury, George, 14
LaPalombara, Joseph G., 79*fn*
Larsen, J. A. O., 44*fn*
Laski, Harold, 10, 16, 17, 104
*Law of Primitive Man, The,* 53*fn*
Lebanon:
  as confessional bureaucracy, 97–101
  quota system in, 133
Legalists, required by bureaucracy, 51
*Legislative System, The,* 24*fn*
Legislators, as representative, 24
Lenin, 34, 49
"Liebermanism," 9